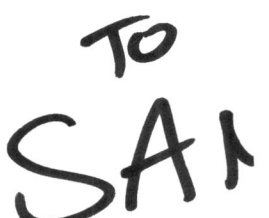

MW01615047

PUPPETRY 101

creating film + television style puppetry

by
ADAM KREUTINGER

illustrations by
IULIAN THOMAS

book cover + layout design by
Cameron Garrity
www.camgarrity.com

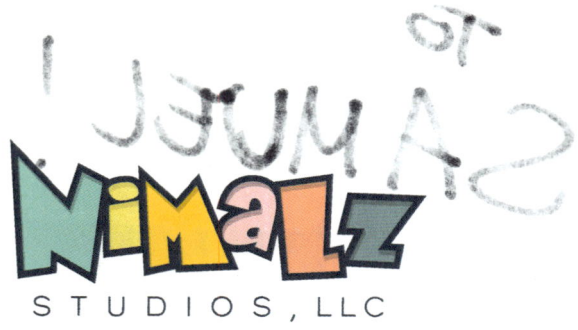

STUDIO, LLC

An Imprint of Nimalz Studios LLC
P.O. Box 774 | Buffalo, NY 14231

© 2022 Nimalz Studios LLC
Nimalz Kidz Books and Publishing is part
of Nimalz Studios LLC

Text © 2022 Adam Kreutinger
Cover and interior illustrations © 2022
Nimalz Studios LLC

ISBN 978-1-959321-03-3

For information about custom editions,
special sales, and premium and corporate purchases,
please contact NimalzKidz@gmail.com.

NimalzStudios.com

Special Thanks **to this book's collaborators**

Aidan Ryan, Andrew Young, Ben Page,
Brian Kenneth Miller, Cameron Garrity, Chase Woolner,
Edna Bland, Jean Marie Keevins, M.Daniel DeCillis,
Sangya Ojha, and Zach Haumesser

TABLE OF CONTENTS

FORWARD
BY DAVE GOELZ, MUPPET PERFORMER

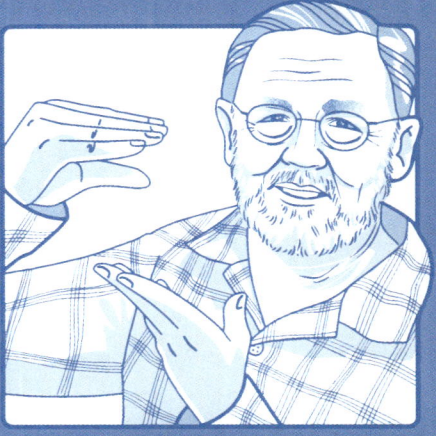

At twenty-six years old, I accidentally started watching the Muppets on *Sesame Street*. After two months, I leaped off my couch and yelled: "I HAVE to have my own Ernie!" At that moment my life changed. I was caught in a tractor beam ... I had to do this!

There was no choice, no escape. I figured out how to build puppets and make videos. Then I met the Muppet people.

That was half a century ago. I never looked back, and I'm still doing it.

Adam Kreutinger is an authority on puppet building and performing techniques. He's an elementary school art teacher who knows how to communicate with kids. He's also an avid puppet builder and performer who produces shows through his company Kreutinger Puppets. Adam's Puppet Nerd YouTube channel shows how to make a variety of puppets. And with

Cameron Garrity, Adam is co-creator of *Puppet Tears*, a podcast featuring in-depth interviews of all sorts of puppet people, including many of the Muppet folk. And if that isn't enough, Adam also runs Camp Puppet, an intensive summer camp program for kids focused on puppets.

And now Adam has written a comprehensive yet precise guide to our style of puppetry. It's written for kids, but it's also valuable for adults. Regardless of your age, if you want to learn about puppetry for the camera, you're in the right place. Somehow, Adam has crammed all the essentials into this book.

Why is puppetry so beguiling? It's because you can be anything. Actors are limited by their appearance as to what they can portray convincingly, but puppeteers can play a person, a clam, a salt shaker. The possibilities are endless: I once played a chill on international television. The only reason I'm still performing after fifty years is that giving life to characters — and celebrating the human condition — is so much fun.

So dive in, and give puppetry a shot! You'll have a lot of fun, and who knows, it could even be the beginning of a whole new life for you.

— Dave Goelz

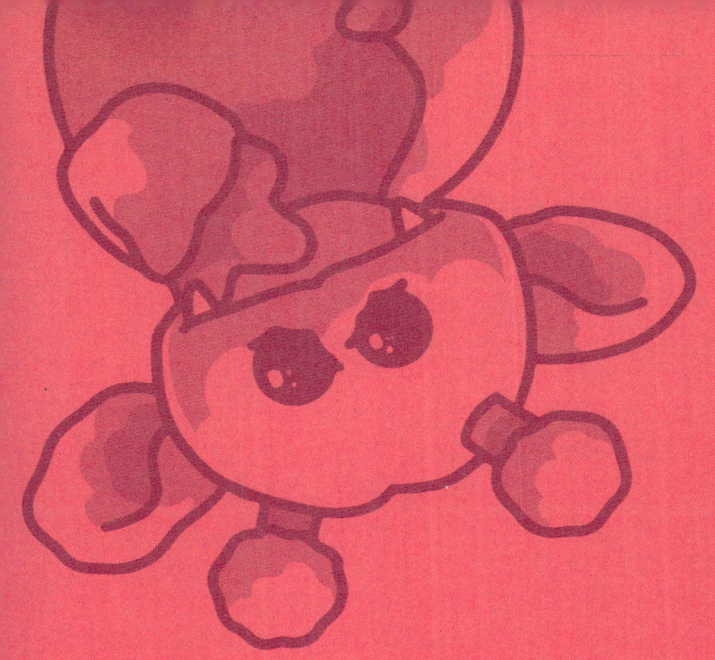

HOW TO USE THIS BOOK

When I was growing up, puppets were just toys. Something I'd see on a rack at the back of the toy store or in a bin at a friend's house mixed in with all the other action figures, dolls, and toy cars. As a kid, there was no such thing as a "puppet show;" a puppet was something you just played with.

When I watched the puppets on *Sesame Street* and the Muppets for the first time, I knew they weren't the same as the puppets I was used to seeing. The characters were so real. I didn't see tags on the back of them or seams running down their faces. Even though those puppets were operated in pretty much the same way as those I saw before, I knew this time

I was seeing something different. That's how I was bitten by the puppetry bug. They were not toys I was seeing onscreen, it was art.

I wanted to be a part of the puppetry magic, but starting was not easy. One of the biggest obstacles I faced getting started in puppetry was the feeling that I needed something else to begin putting a show together — *"As soon as I have (fill in the blank), then I will make the show."* First, I thought that I needed a fancy professional puppet to get started. I spent time and money to make a professional-style puppet, but the feeling that I was lacking something didn't go away. I kept coming up with excuses and moving the goalposts. But my obstacles were imaginary. You can use almost anything as a puppet, and you don't need any skills to start practicing puppetry.

Fortunately, there was a huge puppetry community to learn from and grow with (no strings attached). Inspired by the information I was getting from puppeteers I met on forums and online groups, I gradually began making my own puppets and crafting a show. But even with support, it was hard to get clear guidance on where and how to start. That is why after developing my puppetry skills, I decided to write this book as a sort of shortcut, so you can have a great puppetry experience and create a show with less flailing around than I went through.

Puppetry is awesome. It is an art form that has two lives, sculptural and performative. When you finish a painting, it hangs on a wall. It's pretty much done. But after you spend hours crafting a puppet and it's done, its life has just started. Puppetry includes a little piece of everything

I love: sculpting, sewing, performing, and a touch of magic too. It's an illusion that brings a fur and foam object to life. And best of all, it lets you be anything: a goofy pink alien, a furry blue monkey, or even a banana.

The television style of puppetry that Jim Henson created popularized puppetry and made it mainstream in a way it hadn't been before. Still, before digital devices and the internet, becoming a puppeteer and creating your own show required a ton of resources and gear that was expensive and hard to come by.

Today, it is a different story: creating your own puppet show has never been so accessible to so many people. Whether you want to create a live show to perform at local schools and libraries, or you want to start a YouTube channel to broadcast your show to the world, you can usually get started just by using things you already have at home.

Perhaps you are someone who wants to start their own puppet show. Maybe you have a ton of friends who are interested in puppetry and want to start a puppetry troupe. Maybe you are directing a production of *Little Shop of Horrors* or *Avenue Q* and want to be able to train your actors. Maybe you are a theatre professor and want to teach puppetry in your class. Or maybe you want to make a show and do it all on your own. Whatever goals you have and whatever stage you are currently at in your puppetry career, this book has plenty of resources you can use! By learning from and acknowledging puppetry's history, being inspired by it, and adding your unique voice, you can create high-quality puppetry art and shows that are engaging and memorable.

Even though the focus of this book is a very specific *television* style of puppetry, we cover many other aspects of creating a show that are helpful for planning any style of performance, from educational to entertainment or just plain fun. Aside from the technical skills of performing, we cover the gear you need, how to practice and rehearse, how to write a puppet show, how to promote your show, and more! All these tips will help you not only begin your puppetry adventure, but also create your own unique characters and shows.

The chapters in the book are designed to give some background information, examples, and seeds for your own creativity, so you can get started in puppetry and make a show. By the time you finish, you will no longer be saying, "I want to be a puppeteer." You will say:

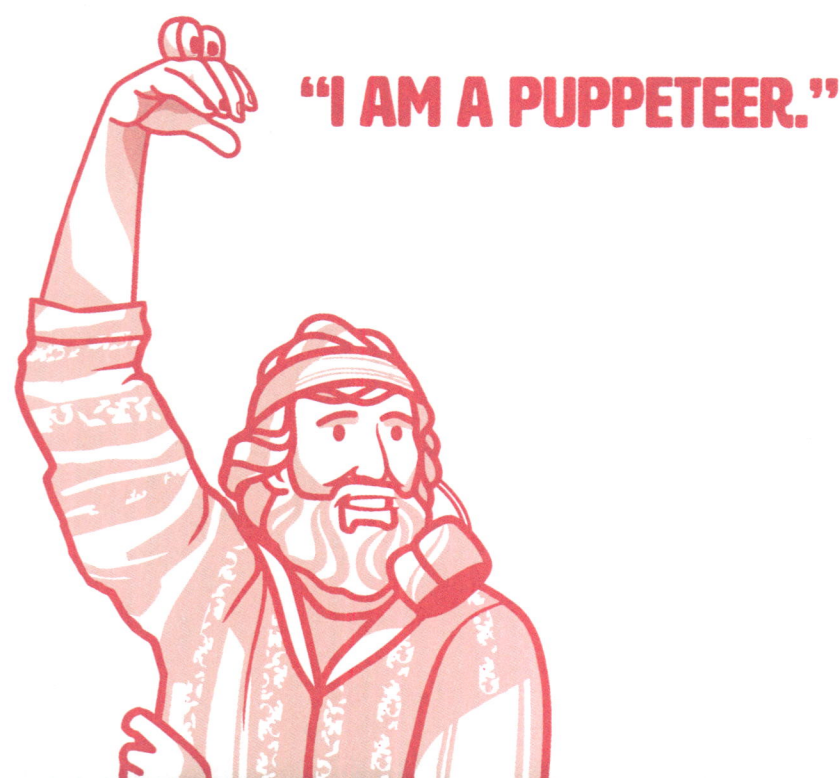

"I AM A PUPPETEER."

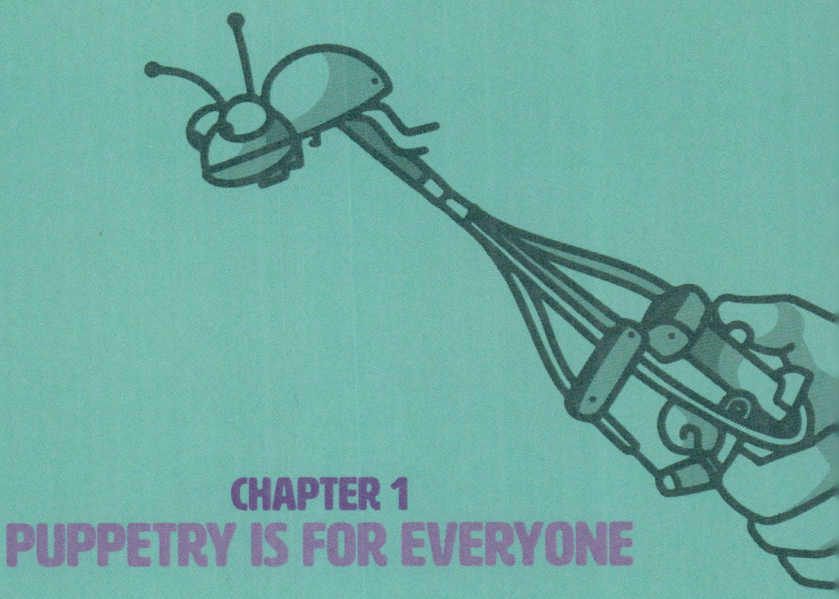

CHAPTER 1
PUPPETRY IS FOR EVERYONE

We're all puppeteers just waiting on a puppet.

According to Josh Kaufman and his viral TEDx talk, "The First 20 Hours – How to Learn Anything", research has shown that within 20 hours, the average person can understand the fundamental mechanics of virtually any skill. For example, if you want to learn how to juggle, first you have to understand the concepts that will allow you to go through the motions (you can't practice until you know what to practice.) Also, Josh Kaufman asserts that to reach proficiency, you need only six months or 10,000 hours to become a top-level expert. So, by the six-month mark, with continual practice, you can consider yourself a puppeteer. And, if you're bitten by the puppetry bug (it's contagious!) and you expand your knowledge and practice with purpose for 10,000 hours – you'll be an absolute master of puppets.

In a way, you may already be a "puppeteer". As a kid, did you ever play with action figures or dolls? Moving these toys around, giving them personalities, and having them talk to each other is definitely puppetry. Or have you ever played a video game? If you think about it, playing video games has many similarities with puppetry. The act of controlling a character on a screen and interacting with a virtual environment much like a set isn't too far off, conceptually, from controlling a puppet on a screen. You are just using your thumbs on a controller to move an image of the character instead of using your arm or full upper body to move a model. And actually, many monster/creature-style puppets from movies are made using wireless servo motors and electronics that are puppeteered using the same sort of controllers as video games use. So, maybe you are using a literal controller to operate your puppet!

SHOOT FOR THE STARS

The thing about puppeteering, is that you can't exactly be bad at it. Actually *puppeteering* comes down to your creative interpretation and your own spin on puppetry. However, it is possible to be a fantastic puppeteer. The first step to achieving that level of success is to look to the greats. They know the tricks; they have the passion – learn from them!

Secondly, practice, practice, practice – rinse and repeat for an unfailing formula for puppetry success! Practice is so important that Chapter 8 is completely dedicated to this topic.

Puppeteering is undeniably fun. From the first moment you see your puppet move to the beat of your drum to when they truly come to life, there will be plenty of laughs, smiles, and fun times along the way. One reason puppetry can be life-changing (for the better) is that it's sustained by a welcoming, dynamic, and highly communicative community that can't wait to meet you! So, why not say hello to them today? You'll find them at local puppetry group meet-ups, on online forums/courses, at puppetry classes, and anywhere else puppetry enthusiasts gather! Chapter 10 is filled with a list of resources for getting involved in the puppetry community.

DON'T HESITATE!

There's no better time to start than right now. And really, what's there to think about? No one has anything to lose by having fun with puppets. On the contrary, it's the perfect way to unwind, keep active, and cultivate a healthy creative outlet.

There are countless resources in this book and at PuppetNerd.com for those interested in learning this entertaining skill. So whether you just want to learn puppetry as a hobby or delve deep into the realm of mastery – this is a great place to get started!

Today's the day to try something new. Who knows – you might fall in love with puppeteering and wonder why you hadn't started earlier! Or worse, you could put it off for years and never pick up a puppet or discover your puppeteering abilities. The world of puppetry awaits you; take the leap! As Henson's most famous character said, "write your own ending" – you've got this!

DON'T WAIT! START NOW!

For most people, the biggest obstacle is not whether or not they should start but where to start. There are so many questions:

What should I do first? Write a script or make a puppet? Should I buy a puppet before I come up with the personality for the character, or should I get the puppet and then discover its characteristics from there?

Though there isn't a "right" or "wrong" way to start, I do have a few recommendations. If you are stuck on where to start, you should start with what you already know. Getting the "easy stuff" done first will give you confidence in moving forward with the other aspects of the project. You can learn what you don't know by starting with what you do know. Which skills do you already have and are best at?

On the one hand, if writing comes easily, start with some scripts. This can come in handy and save you a ton of time in the future. Having a script before any sets and puppets are built allows you the most freedom to take your story in any direction you want. Also, a script can be a perfect guide that lets you know exactly what needs to be in your show.

On the other hand, if you have crafting skills and are good at making things, having the physical sets or a puppet in your hands can be extremely motivational in getting a project moving. Sometimes by simply creating some props and a character, the story starts to write itself.

For example, if you made a pig puppet and a talking slice of cake puppet, there is inherently a story there with some comedy in it. The built-in conflict – the pig is hungry, and the cake doesn't want to be eaten – automatically makes the story interesting. However, you don't have to go with the obvious choice for a story. If you really want to throw your audience for a loop, have the skit end with the cake eating the pig!

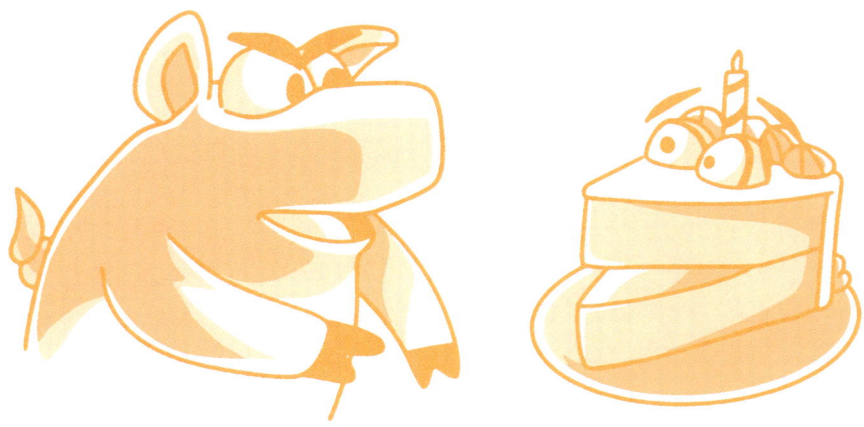

On the other hand (that's three hands for those of you who are counting – a puppeteer's dream!) maybe you like to sing or write music or lyrics. Puppets and music go together really well. A single song can serve as the inspiration for an entire story. In fact, there have been many movies and musicals that have been inspired by just one song. Not only that, but a song can even be an entire story. Who doesn't love a good music video?

The Muppets are a perfect example of the combination of music and puppets. They have countless original songs that are extremely popular, not to mention covers of famous songs by others – one of their most popular music videos ever was a cover of the song Bohemian Rhapsody by Queen.

So whether you are writing original songs or stringing together a bunch of classics to make a jukebox musical, music is a great way to tell a story.

WHEN IN DOUBT, PLAY

If you feel like you don't have any of the above skills that make a good starting point for creating a puppet show, that is okay. None of those skills are a prerequisite for making your own puppet show. If you don't know where to begin, then playing is the perfect way to start.

Play is a great way to generate ideas because it's proactive. Start with a sock or a paper bag puppet. Or even draw eyes on your hand and start to make it talk.

Though it is not necessary, having other people for your puppet to interact with can help too. Whether it's a friend or family member, young or old, you might be surprised by how much fun it is. Just having a simple conversation with the puppet can spark plenty of ideas and even start to create or solidify the puppet's personality.

If you do not have anyone for your puppet to interact with, turn on the television and have your puppet do some commentary, or maybe have your puppet do a movie review. The point is to get your puppet talking and showing its personality as much as you can. The more you get your character talking and reacting to different situations, the more clear it will be what kinds of skits and stories would fit well with them.

FORGET ABOUT WHAT-IFS

Don't be afraid to fail. Failure is inevitable along the way. No one ever learned anything without getting it wrong first. It's all part and parcel of gaining invaluable experience and honing in on your talents. Think of any mistake you make along your puppetry journey as a learning experience.

CHAPTER 1 TAKEAWAYS

- The best time to start is now

- Start with your strengths

- Remember to have fun and play. It can spark inspiration.

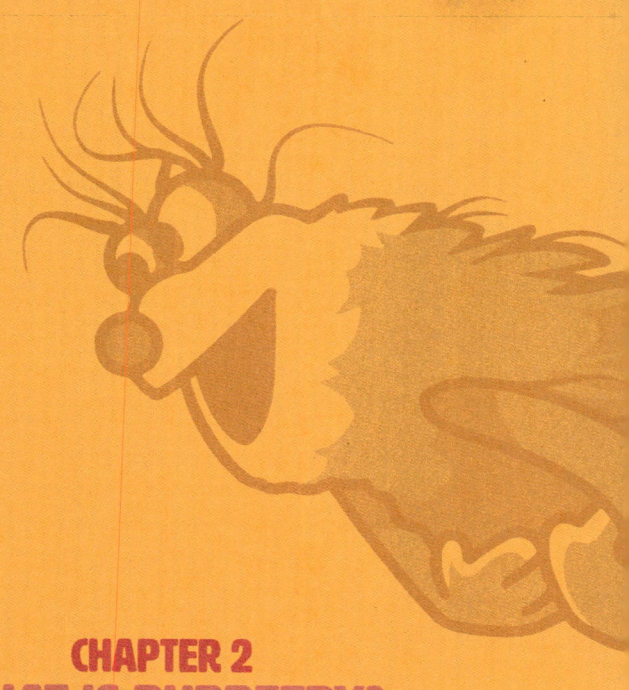

CHAPTER 2
WHAT IS PUPPETRY?

Many people define puppetry as "creating the illusion of life in an inanimate object." This is how I used to define puppetry too. But the more I learn about puppetry and explore the artform, the more I feel like this technical definition doesn't quite cover it. Puppetry is very diverse, and often you don't even need a puppet to put on a show.

For example, the remarkable Peruvian puppeteers Hugo and Ines don't do puppetry in a way you might expect. They are renowned for combining mime and puppetry to perform characters using their hands, knees, nose, and feet rather than inanimate objects.

I'll never forget seeing them perform at the National Puppetry Conference at the Eugene O'Neill Theater

Center. Their level of creativity was so inspiring. I already knew there were many different forms of puppetry, but I had never seen anything like this show. It was magic.

The aspect of their work I love the most is how they create characters right before the audience's eyes. For example, Ines walked onto the stage, laid down and raised her foot into the air. Then piece by piece, the character would slowly take form as if it was getting ready for the day: putting on a shirt, combing toes as if to style its hair, and putting a hat on. Frankly this puppet had more personality than most people I know.

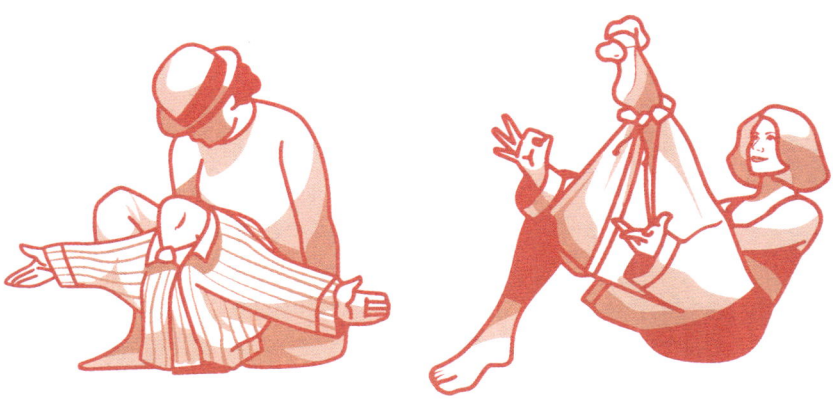

Puppetry also can be done by just using hands. Bob Stromberg can make hyper-realistic shadow puppets. Each character he is able to create is so detailed that it is hard to believe he is not using anything other than his hands. And even more impressive is how quickly he can switch from character to character. During a live performance, it looks like the shadows are morphing right before your eyes.

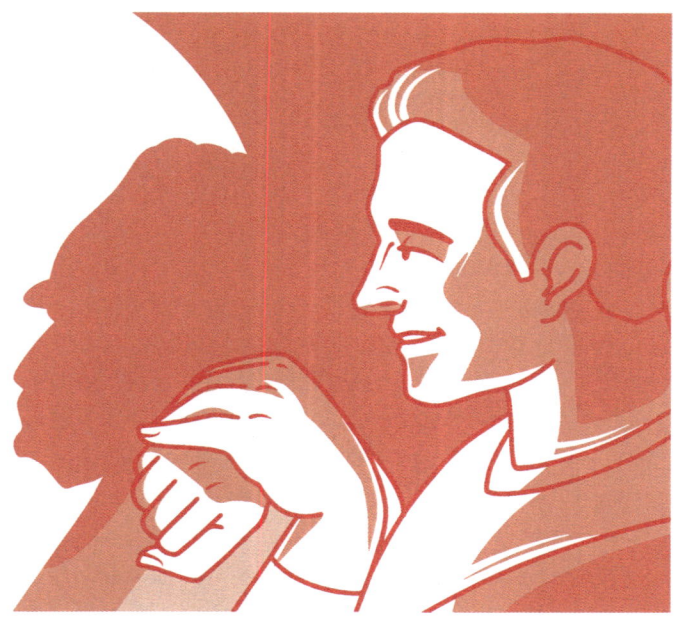

So whether it's Bob Stromberg's hands, Hugo's knee, Ines's foot, or something else completely original, unforgettable puppetry can be created without even using a puppet.

For these reasons, I define puppetry as intentionally creating a personality or the illusion of consciousness in *anything*. Thus, anything can be a puppet, and consequently anyone can be a puppeteer. So whether you are using a traditional puppet, object manipulation, or body movement, you are part of the world of puppetry.

FINDING THE RIGHT PUPPET FOR YOU

There are many different kinds of puppets used today. From tabletop to toy theater and shadow puppets to marionettes, there are tons of styles and types of puppets. And honestly, it can get a little confusing to keep them all straight. Some of the names are so generic that they could easily apply to multiple kinds of puppets. For instance, I often see people referring to *live-hand puppets* as *glove puppets* and referring to *glove puppets* as *hand puppets*, and so on. When you know the difference, the confusion is understandable.

To keep things clear, in this book, we are going to focus on the television style of puppetry developed by Jim Henson. From here on, we will refer to this style as "television puppetry" and the characters as "television puppets".

THERE ARE A FEW DIFFERENT STYLES OF TELEVISION PUPPETS

- Hand-rod puppets
- Live hand and sack puppets
- Walkaround puppets
- Mech (mechanical) puppets

These are the main types of puppets made for the screen. No matter what puppet show you watch, you'll be able to spot at least one of these variations of a puppet, and maybe all of them. Let's break down the differences.

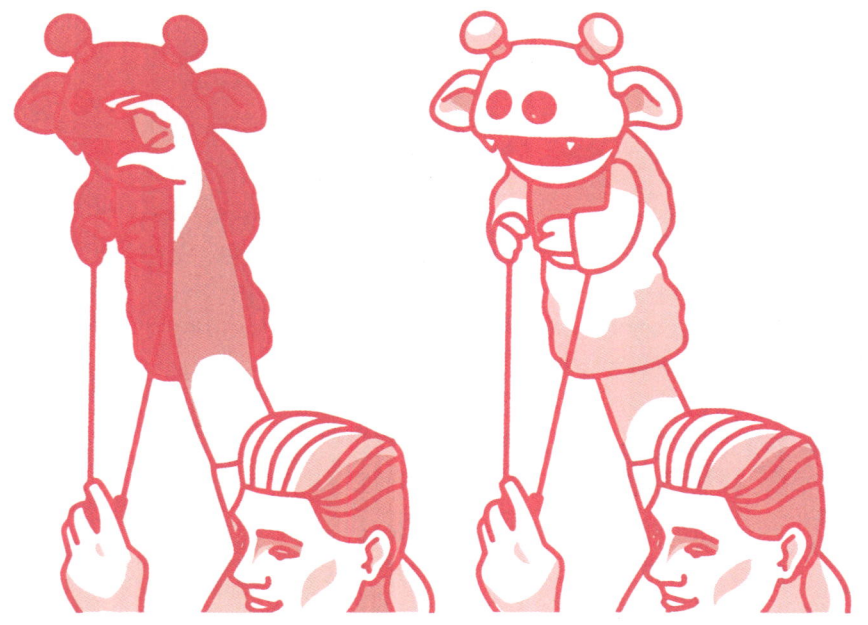

HAND-ROD PUPPETS

Typically, a single puppeteer can control a hand-rod puppet with both hands. The puppeteer's dominant hand goes into the base of the puppet all the way up to its head. This hand position allows the puppeteer to operate the mouth of the puppet effectively. To control the puppet's limbs, the performer's other hand uses the arm rods, thin metal rods connected to the puppet's wrists.

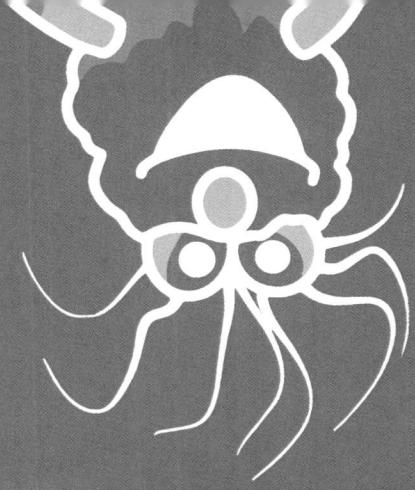

LIVE-HAND & SACK PUPPETS

The next type is the live-hand puppet. This puppet involves two puppeteers to operate fully. Generally, the main puppeteer positions their dominant hand at the base of the puppet's head, while their less dominant hand goes into one of the puppet's arms. The second puppeteer controls the second hand of the puppet. Here, there are no arm rods. Instead, you slide your hands into the arm of the puppet like into a glove to operate the puppet's hands directly.

Sometimes, the main puppeteer will perform only the head while the second puppeteer operates both hands. This arrangement is especially handy if your puppet's hands need to be even more coordinated while doing some intricate task such as drumming or another activity that requires rhythm.

If you need to perform a live hand puppet by yourself, you can stuff the extra arm with filling and pin it to the puppet's body so it doesn't swing around loosely during the performance.

Most of the time, live-hand puppets have only four fingers. In this case, the performers' ring finger and pinky go together into the pinky of the puppet's hand.

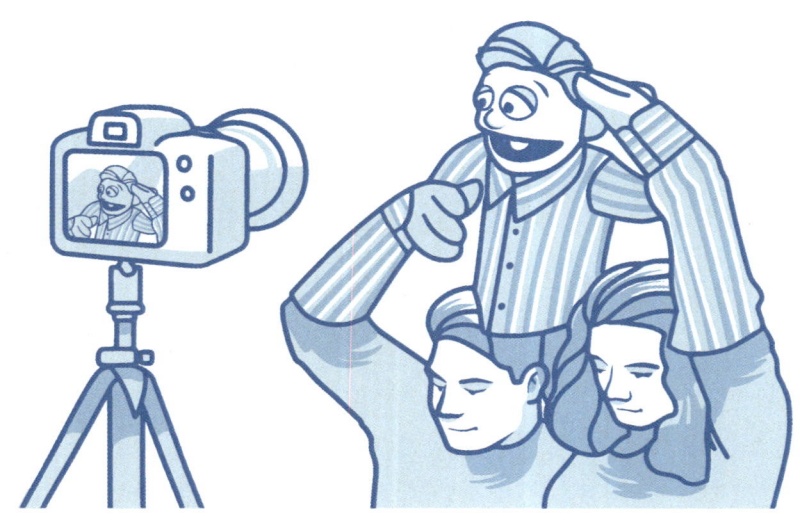

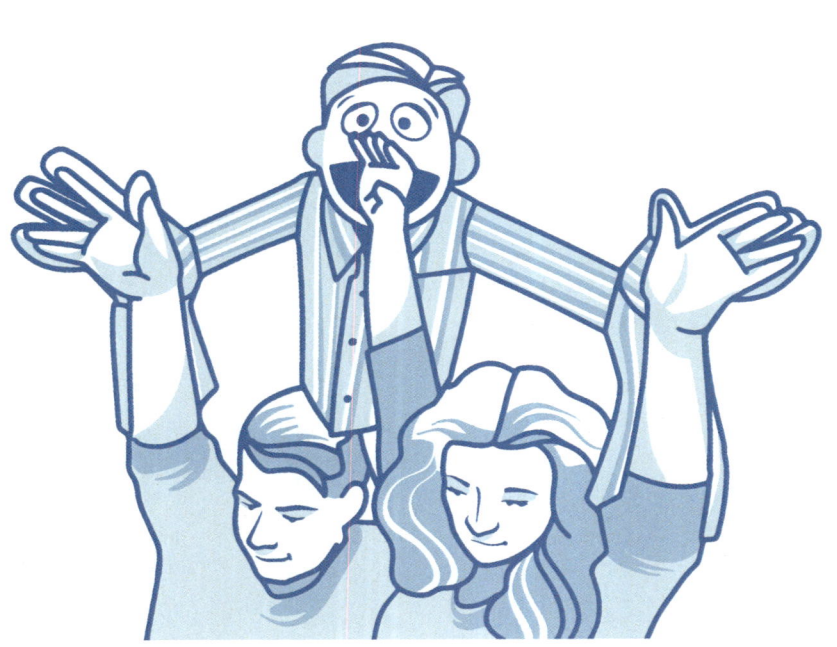

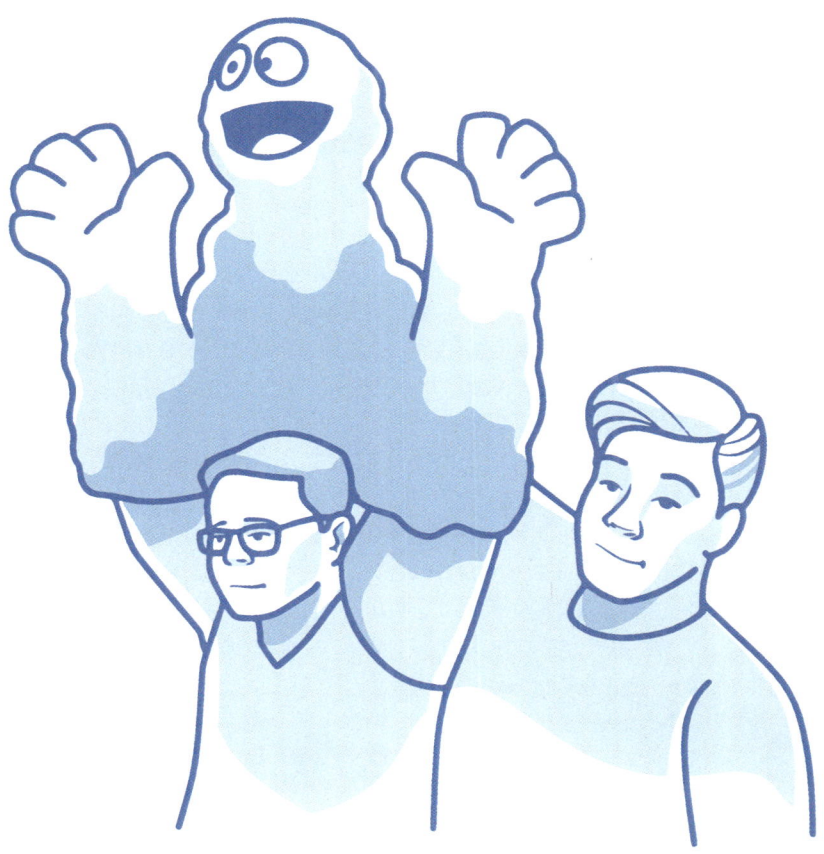

There is another form of live hand puppet known as a sack puppet. A sack puppet is operated the same way as a live hand puppet, except there are no separate entrance holes for each arm. Instead, there is one large entrance at the bottom of the puppet. This can make the puppet seem very large and is great for any big fur-covered animal or monster puppet.

WALKAROUND PUPPETS

Another style of puppet is a full-bodied walkaround puppet. This puppet combines the idea of a walkaround mascot costume with puppetry.

Typically, from shoulders down, the character is a costume with the puppeteer inside of it. The head is most often controlled by one of the performer's hands inside the costume, while the other hand controls one of the arms. The second arm of the puppet is usually either pinned to the body so it doesn't swing around or attached to a string that loops through the neck of the puppet to the other arm. The second arrangement allows the puppeteer to move both arms but in the opposite way. When you raise one arm, the other goes down, and vice-versa. If you have an oversized character, a full-bodied puppet is necessary to effectively deliver the illusion.

One challenge in full-bodied puppets is devising a way for the puppeteer to be able to see. In some cases, there is a small hole or piece of see-through mesh material somewhere on the puppet for the performer to see through. Other times, especially on the set of a TV show or movie, the puppeteer will have a small TV monitor strapped to their chest to have an outside view.

It can be a view of the performance from the view of the audience like traditional television puppetry using a monitor, or a small camera can even be positioned on or in the puppet's head so the puppeteer can see from the puppet's point of view.

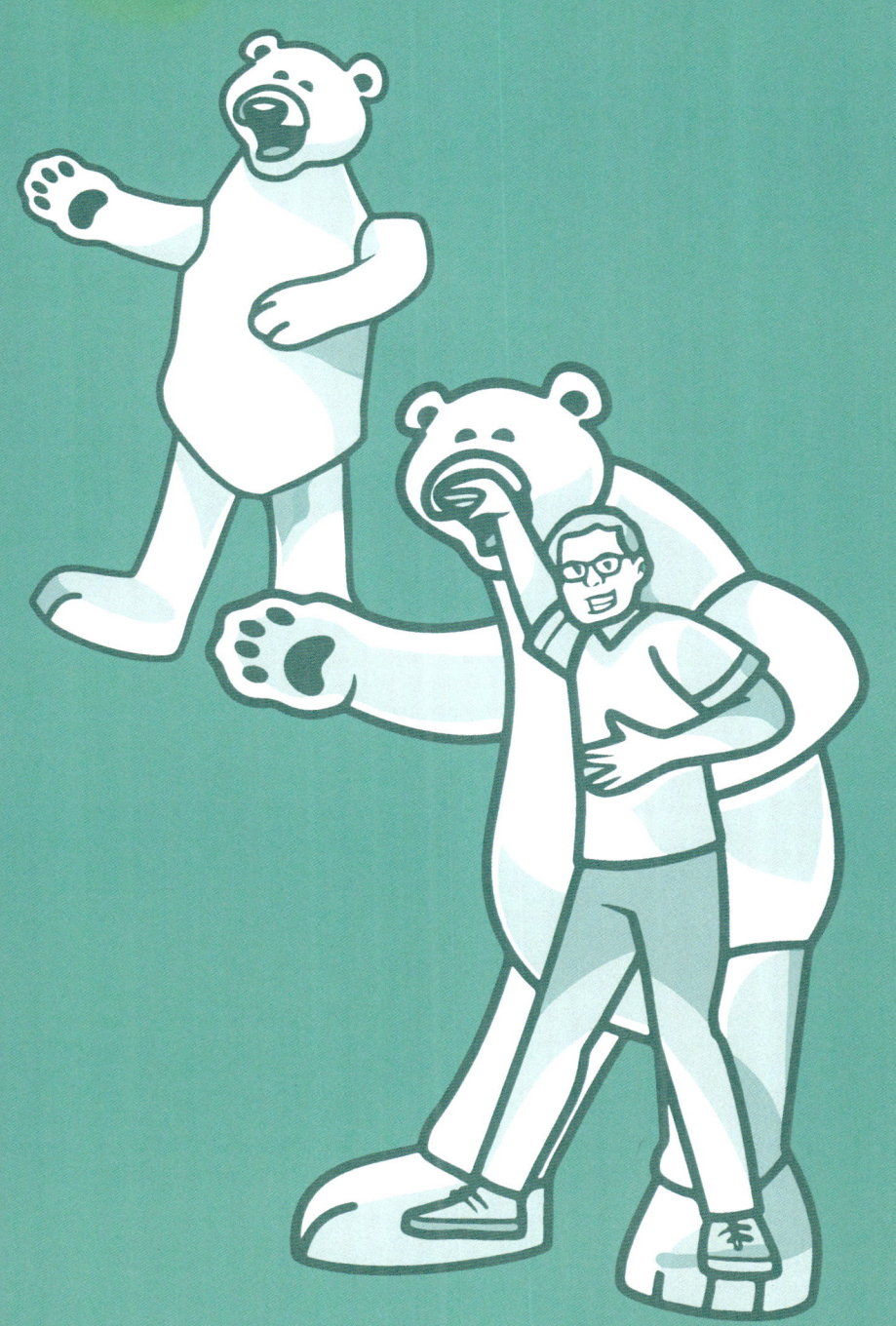

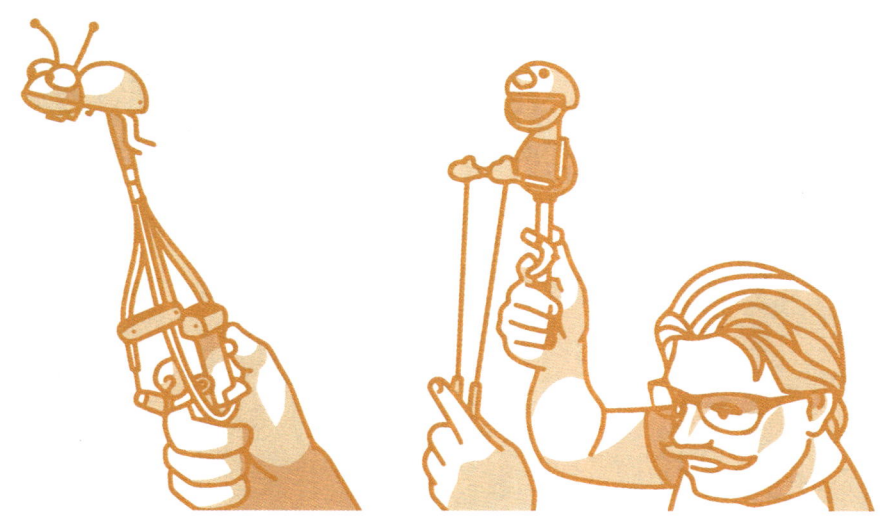

MECH PUPPET

The "mech" in the mech puppet stands for "mechanism". This puppet is completely or partially controlled with strings, cables, or some combination; it is sometimes even wirelessly controlled.

There are a few reasons to use mechanisms in puppets. Sometimes a puppet is so small that your hand just can't fit inside it. Having springs, strings, and hinges inside the puppet can allow you to perform a small character like this.

Another reason to use mechs in a puppet is to add expression. Whether it's blinking eyes, retracting teeth or wiggling ears, these types of additions can add a lot of character to your puppets. But it's important to remember that overuse of mechs may come off more like a gimmick rather than a tool to enhance the character or story you are telling.

Sometimes mechanisms are necessary to achieve a particular effect or to operate a puppet in a location where it is impossible to fit a performer. If a puppet needs to ride a bike, for instance, you might use a wireless remote or another mechanism.

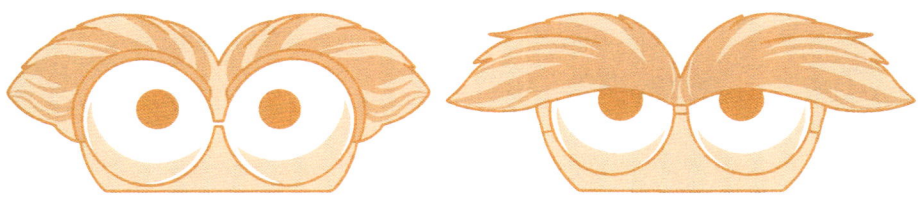

TELEVISION PUPPETS

These styles of Television Puppets are the most common. The type of Television Puppet that fits the character you want to perform will depend on what your puppet needs to do and on the character design you have in mind.

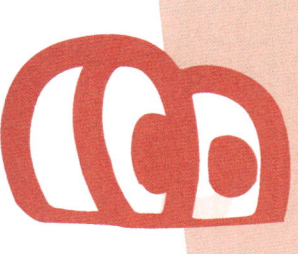

PRO TIP!
Next time you are watching a puppet show on TV, see if you can guess which type of puppet is being used.

Creating your own signature character is easier said than done. However, when in doubt, just start. It may seem blunt, but hey, it worked for Jim Henson.

Did you know that despite his present-day superstar status, Kermit the Frog has some very unglamorous origins? Jim Henson made the first Kermit puppet from a few ping pong balls and a green coat he borrowed from his mother. Who would have thought a DIY frog would become one of the most iconic characters in television history? But that's the beauty of creation, acting, and imagination – anything goes, especially in puppetry. So, now all you need is a puppet.

In the next chapter, we're going to learn specific techniques for operating puppets and bringing them to life.

CHAPTER 2 TAKEAWAYS

- Anything can be a puppet; you are only limited by your imagination.
- Think about why your character might be better as a live hand versus a rod puppet. Or a mech puppet instead of a live hand puppet.
- Pick a style of puppet that fits your needs.

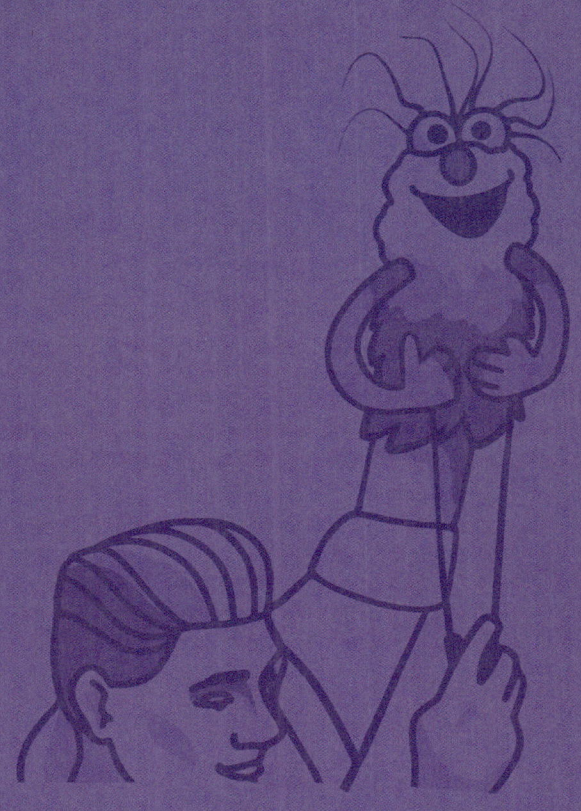

CHAPTER 3
HOW TO PUPPETEER!

Even though puppetry might look like kids' stuff, it is not easy. Learning to puppeteer like a pro takes a lot of practice. In this chapter, we will focus on the technical skills needed to make a television puppet come to life. (Many of these techniques can be applied to other forms of puppetry, too.)

Control is a fundamental aspect of puppetry. Anyone can wave and wiggle a puppet around, but puppeteers are in full control of the puppet's movements. Manipulating your puppets with intention and being fully aware of your performance and what you are trying to portray to the audience with your puppet character is how you master control of your character.

So, how do you learn control? Part of control is understanding and mastering the manipulation techniques: *eye focus*, *lip-sync*, *ground*, *entrances and exits*, *puppet's arms*, and even the *Henson Punch*. These techniques are like tools in your toolbox. You have to know how to use your puppetry tools to put on a great show. It's a good idea to practice these manipulation techniques as much as you can before jumping into a performance, or else you will risk developing bad habits in your performance. Picking up bad habits when you are first learning puppetry is the last thing you want to do. That is why maintaining control is so important. Without a doubt, there is a looseness to having a natural puppet performance. But as the saying goes, you have to learn to walk before you can run.

Let's take a look at what's involved with these techniques.

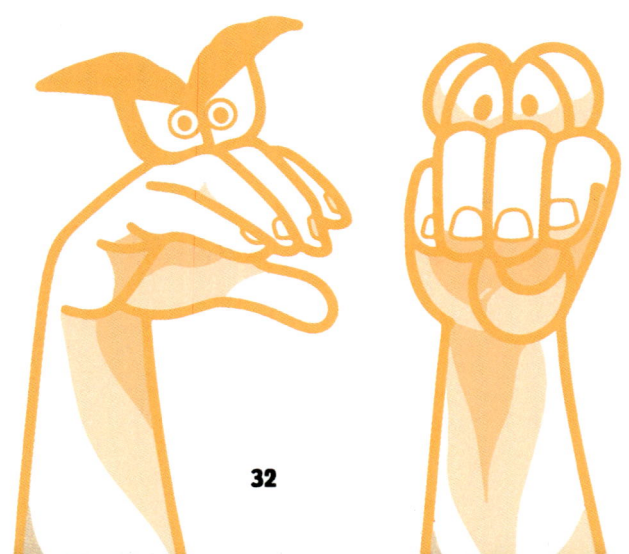

EYE FOCUS

In my eyes (pun intended), eye focus is the most important technique for creating a believable performance. Most people seem to think lip-sync is most important, but this isn't so. This is because puppets are not always talking, but they are always looking at something. Propper eye focus is what makes your character really seem alive.

Eye focus is especially important when filming puppets and using a monitor because it allows your character to make a connection with the audience. When we as humans are talking to someone, we tend to look each other in the eyes. This is natural in conversations, and it is what makes puppets seem alive. When eye contact is absent, we feel that something is off.

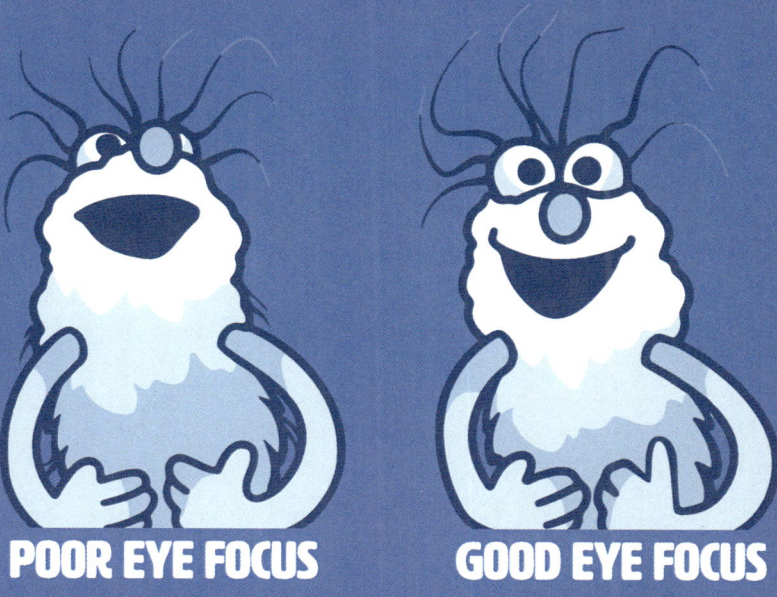

POOR EYE FOCUS   **GOOD EYE FOCUS**

PRO TIP!
Find an episode of *Sesame Street* on YouTube and watch one scene, but only pay attention to the puppets who **aren't** speaking. Notice their eyes, where they're looking, how they're moving. See how they're still engaged, even when they're not talking? That's what we're going for.

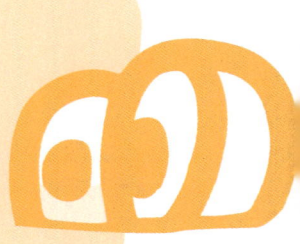

For example, imagine you are at a café having a smoothie with a friend and chatting about your day. If they were looking at the ceiling the whole time they were talking and never really made eye contact with you the way they usually do, you might think something unusual was going on. I'm sure you would not get more than a minute into the conversation without being distracted by this and asking them if they are okay.

Eye focus is especially important when multiple puppets are in a scene together. To keep a scene looking natural, all puppets must have correct eye focus. Even if one puppeteer is maintaining proper eye focus, if another character is not looking in the right direction, it would be distracting to the audience and could spoil the whole scene.

An extra tip for eye focus when using a monitor is to make sure both pupils are visible at all times. We will cover more specifics on using a monitor in Chapter 6. If a puppet is in a complete side profile view and you can only see one pupil, the illusion of life seems to fade away. But by adding a slight head tilt instead with a three-quarter turn, you achieve the effect of the puppet looking to the side without it being in full profile. This position helps make the character feel more alive. The eyes are the gateway to what makes the puppet a believable character; try to keep them visible whenever possible.

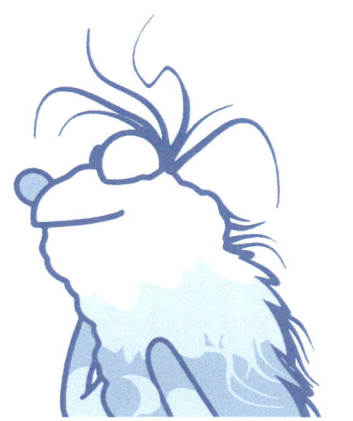

SIDE VIEW FULL PROFILE

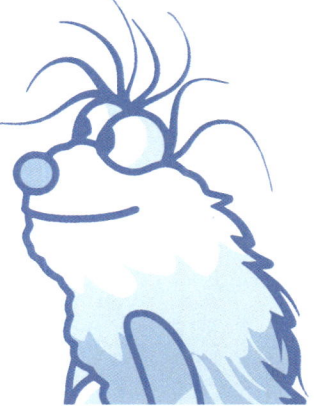

SIDE VIEW SLIGHT TILT

It is impossible to know for sure if your character has proper eye focus if you are not using a monitor. Looking up at your puppet does not give you the correct vantage point to know for sure. If you find yourself in a situation where it's not possible to use a monitor, here is a simple tip. Using your hand that is inside the puppet's head, point your finger at what your character is looking at. Depending on the fit of your puppet, this should get your eye focus close to what you want, and might be your only option if you are in the background of a large group scene. The best way to maintain good eye focus is to be mindful of it.

LIP-SYNC

Generally, the puppet's mouth should open once for each syllable. Knowing and sticking to this simple rule is a great place to start when learning lip-sync for a puppet. However, if you watch a lot of television puppetry, you will notice that this is not the only way of doing lip-sync. Techniques for lip-sync will vary depending on the speed and rhythm of the dialogue.

If the puppet character is speaking slowly, you will stick to opening the mouth for each syllable. But if you try to hit every syllable when the character is talking really fast, it will not look natural. It makes the performance look too mechanical and has too much movement. I call this "motormouth". When you are doing motormouth lip-sync, your puppet will not feel alive.

If the character is talking fast, you will generally open the mouth fewer times, just hitting important beats. For example, if your puppet says, "Hello, I like puppetry", that phrase has 7 syllables. Let's break down how to perform the lip-sync if you were doing it slowly and how it might look fast.

If puppeteered slowly, the phrase will be broken into 7 beats and look like this:

"HELL-O, I LIKE PUP-PET-TRY"

However, if your character is excited or angry, they might be yelling faster. In this case, the phrase would be broken into five beats:

"HELLO, I LIKE PUPPET-TRY"

Switching back and forth between these two types of lip-sync might seem straightforward, but it can take a while to learn how to do it seamlessly. The goal is to make this switch second nature. You want to be able to focus 100% on the emotions and feelings your character is going through, so it is important to practice the lip-sync techniques till you can do this without having to think about it.

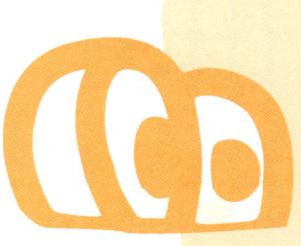

PRO TIP!

Practice lip-syncing while you are talking on the phone. Have your hand match what you are saying. This is a great way to get some extra practice in – and the person on the other end of the call will never even know!

DROP THE JAW

In addition to hitting the syllables, dropping the jaw is another major pillar in what it takes to have perfect lip-sync for your puppet. This may seem obvious, but it is actually not the first instinct of most beginner puppeteers. To make the puppet talk, the instinct of most people is to lift their fingers up to form the words the character is saying. For comparison, if you wanted to mimic that action with your own head when talking, instead of dropping your jaw to talk, you would have to throw your head back on each mouth movement you made. This is not natural.

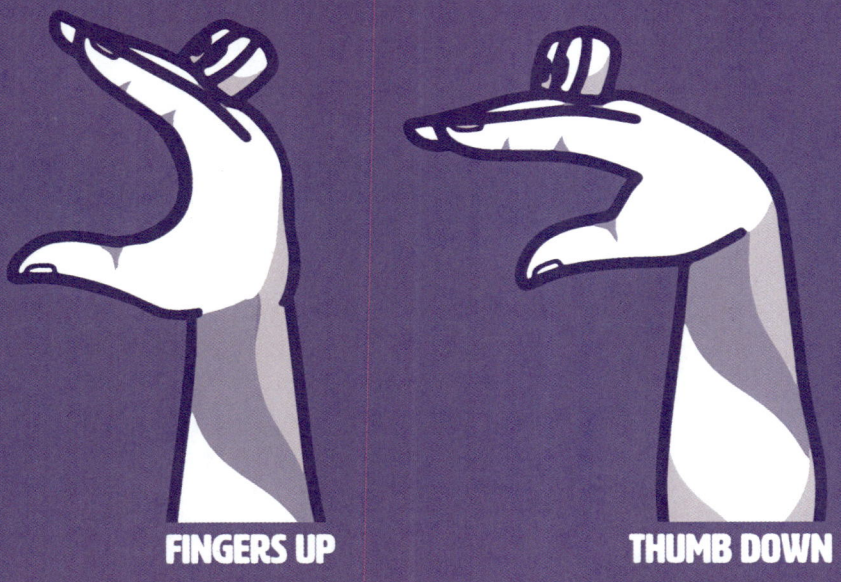

FINGERS UP   **THUMB DOWN**

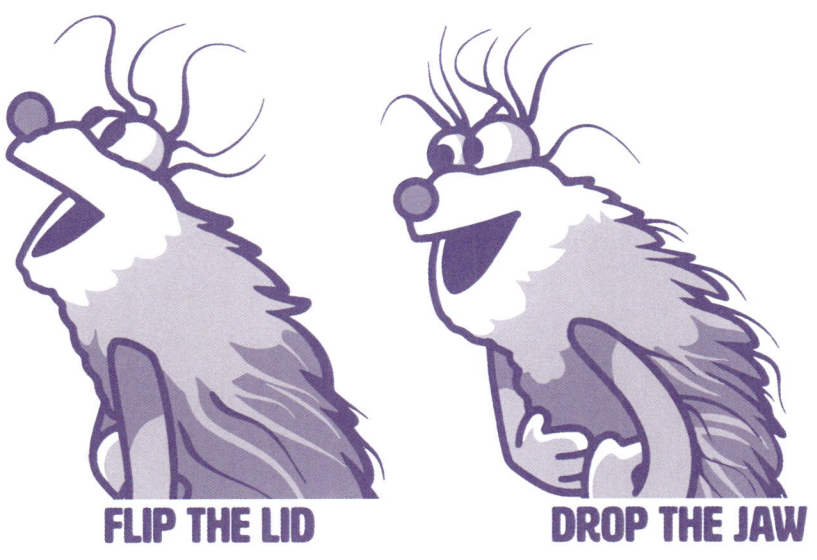

FLIP THE LID   ## DROP THE JAW

Lifting fingers up is called "flipping the lid". Not only is this clearly unnatural, it also makes it impossible to give your puppet propper eye focus while talking. Your character cannot look into the camera or at another puppet if their eyes are flapping up at the ceiling with each movement of their mouth.

In order to correct this, you need to instead drop your thumb to make the bottom jaw go down so you can keep your eye focus locked. Otherwise, your character will look like it is always yelling and not be able to make a connection with the audience.

THINGS TO AVOID WHEN LEARNING LIP-SYNC

Probably the most common mistake people make with lip-sync when first trying on a puppet is "biting the words." Biting the words is when you are accidentally closing the mouth on each beat instead of opening it. This is quite literally the opposite action that should be taking place, and it's important to correct this mistake as soon as possible to avoid it becoming a habit. A simple tip to prevent "biting the words" is to make sure to keep the puppet's mouth closed before you start talking.

Another thing to avoid is strain in your hand. Though your hand might be in different positions depending on the design of your puppet, it should be as comfortable and relaxed as possible. There are two poor hand postures I often see in new puppeteers. One is having a wrist bent down too far. Your wrist should not be at a 90-degree angle during a performance as this is an unnatural position for your hand that could cause injury. The only time when you should bend your wrist more is when your character is looking down for a moment.

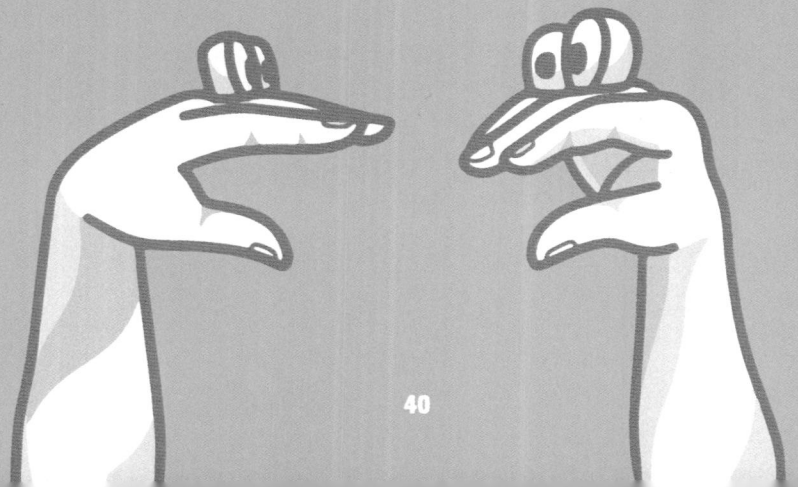

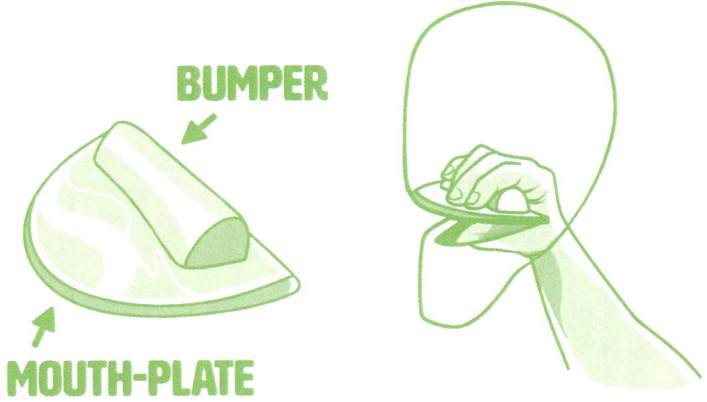

BUMPER

MOUTH-PLATE

The second poor hand posture I see is "flat fingers." Again, there might be moments where this position is appropriate depending on the expression you are trying to make, but it should not be a neutral or default position. It is best to have your fingers gently curled. If your puppet's mouth plate has a bumper in it (see the figure above), your fingers will be in a curled position naturally. However, many puppets do not have that type of mouth grip, so you will want to make sure you are not straining your fingers. A long day doing puppetry might end with some sore muscles, but it is important to not put unneeded strain on your wrist and finger joints.

WHAT IS A BUMPER?

A bumper is a small grip inside the mouth plate of some puppets. Having a bumper in your puppet can prevent the feeling that a puppet is slipping off your hand and it can sometimes help you to create certain expressions with your puppet's face.

THE HENSON PUNCH

Earlier, we clearly established the importance of dropping your thumb when making your puppet talk. However, another technique Jim Henson developed takes this skill to the next level. When Jim performs his characters, he is doing more than just dropping his thumb; his technique really makes it feel like the words are actually coming out of the character's mouth.

This technique—"The Henson Punch"—involves bending your wrist down as you open your hand. You want to almost act as if you are throwing the words out of your hand. This movement can be done subtly when the character is talking normally, but it is even more effective when the puppet is excited and showing a lot of emotion. It is also common for performers to use this technique to keep their wrists loose, giving the puppets' heads a subtle side-to-side tilt, which is especially engaging for film puppetry.

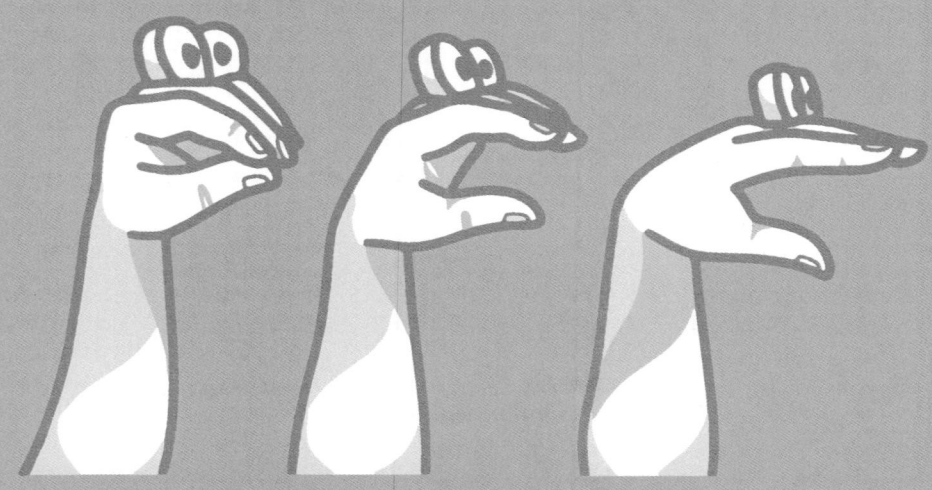

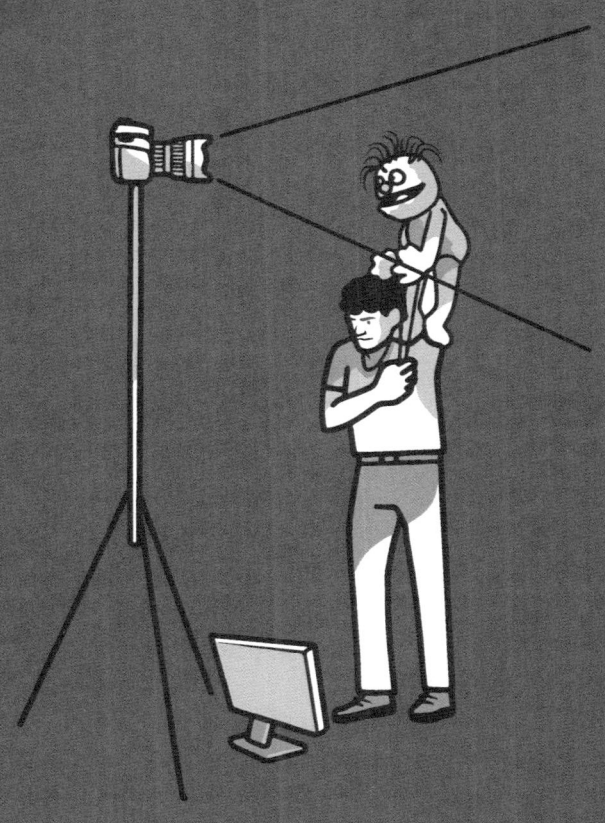

GROUND

It is often thought that puppeteers have to be sewn into a couch or scrunched up behind a set piece to stay out of view. Though this belief may be true for some situations, in television puppetry, the characters are typically performed over the puppeteer's head while they stand. To accommodate this setup, many professional television puppet shows use a raised set; this is when all the set pieces and backgrounds are held high on stilts. But since the camera is also raised high up, everything being filmed looks normal and as it should.

The big advantage of using a raised set is that it allows the puppeteers much more mobility. Rather than walking on their knees or scooting around on their bottom, a raised set lets them walk around freely. Not only is this a safer environment to perform in, but it is also much less of a strain, allowing the puppeteer to focus more on staying in character than worrying about where their body is. It also helps the puppeteer move faster on their feet, making it easier for them to make the puppet run or skate in and out of the frame of the camera.

However, a raised set brings a unique set of challenges too. Since the camera and the set are typically raised, the puppets' feet (if they even have feet) are of course very far away from actually touching the ground. So, a puppeteer needs to trick the camera and make it look like their puppet is standing on solid ground. In other words, you need to give your puppet "Ground". **Ground is creating the illusion that a character is standing or walking when their waist is below the frame.**

It is common for a new puppeteer to accidentally have their puppet drift around the screen. Sometimes the character will even look like it is in quicksand and slowly sink as the puppeteer's arm gets tired.

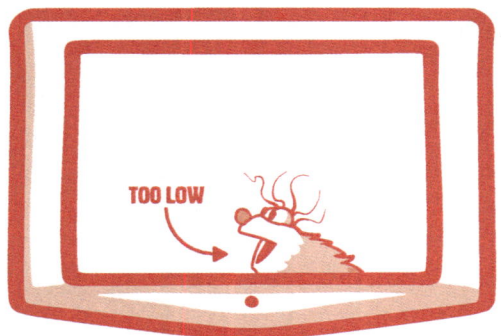

Other times the puppeteer will have their puppet held up too high, and their arm or even their head may be showing in the shot. Or sometimes, when the puppet enters from the side, a beginner will accidently have their puppet slide into the shot instead of making it look like the puppet walks in.

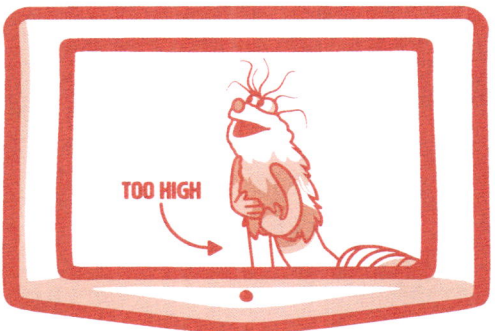

Be sure your character doesn't look like it is floating around. Maintain control of your performance. You can create the illusion of walking by gently bouncing your arm as your puppet moves across the frame. Your character should look as natural as a human actor walking around a set.

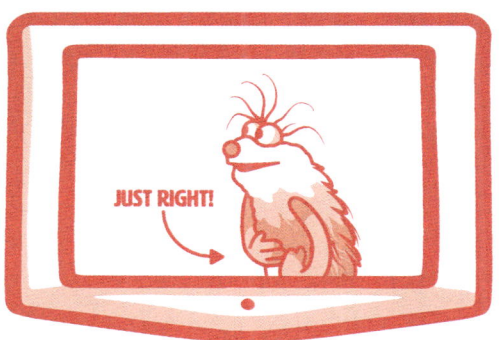

Since puppets go well with music, they often have to dance. Effective puppet choreography can be simple. Just move your puppet body to the right and both arms to the left. Then reverse it, moving the puppet to the left and its arms to the right. Continue this back and forth to the beat of the music, and you have a dancing puppet!

ENTRANCES & EXITS

Now we know giving your puppet ground creates the illusion of the character standing and walking. This is easy enough to remember when you are in the middle of a scene. But in the excitement of starting or finishing a scene, it can be easy to forget. You must make sure to maintain the illusion the entire time.

Your puppet entering the scene is the audience's first impression of them. If your character just floats in, it can be hard to regain a sense of realism no matter what your character says or does. Also, the way a character exits and enters can say a lot about them. If your puppet stomps in with a scrunched face, we already have a good idea of their mood or attitude before they even open their mouth. Thus, entrances and exits are a great way to continue to develop your character's personality.

PUPPET ARMS

Whether your character has arm rods or live hands, it is crucial that the puppet's arm movements look natural, even when they're at rest. When using rods, beginner puppeteers make the mistake of keeping the puppet's arms in an unnatural position by resting them below the puppet's chin.

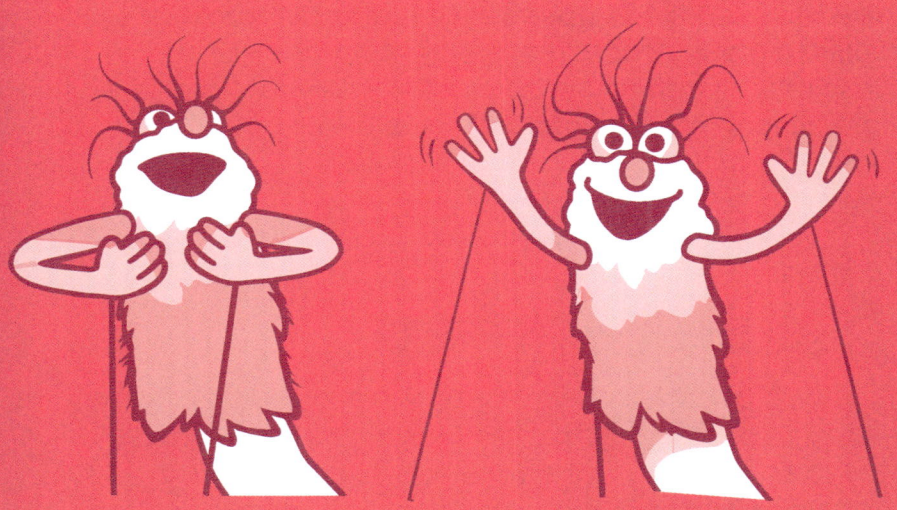

Another common problem I see is having the hands do too much, especially with live hand puppets. A lot of beginners feel that if their puppet's hands aren't doing something then they are not doing puppetry. This instinct can be hard to overcome. However, keeping the arms of your puppet looking natural is a major step in achieving the illusion of life in your puppet. The downbeats of a character patiently listening, thinking, and waiting are what truly makes the puppets feel like they are alive.

If you are making a puppet video, I challenge you to maintain this illusion even if you make a mistake that requires you to do another take. Imagine your puppet saying the wrong word, acknowledging it, and running off camera to get reset for the next take. Performing your puppetry like this, as if the puppet were a real actor, would make a great blooper reel giving you more inspiration for the content and also lets you get deeper into your puppet's personality.

PUTTING IT ALL TOGETHER

With practice and awareness, you can add subtleties in your performance that can truly bring a puppet to life. Just like acting, you can really draw an audience in when your performance is natural rather than overacting. However, many people's first instinct with a puppet is just that: everything tends to be over-exaggerated.

Audiences can accidentally encourage this type of performance, too. Maybe you shook a puppet with the mouth open and let its arms flail and flap around, and the audience laughed. It feels good to "get a laugh". A positive reaction from the audience is a great affirmation that makes you want to repeat the same action. But it is also important to think critically about why they are laughing. Is it because they believe the illusion that this character is alive—and the puppet is earning the laughs? Or are they laughing because the illusion is broken and it's funny that a person is shaking a doll?

If something gets laughs, that doesn't mean it's actually good. It could be that they are just reacting to it because it was unexpected or cringy. You can't always rely on a laugh being precise feedback from the audience. Your performance has to be good on its own.

I'm not saying there is never a reason to break the fourth wall in the context of a show. Perhaps you have written a story where the audience is supposed to realize they are watching a puppet show. But if you want the audience to believe that your character is alive, I wouldn't recommend it.

To achieve the illusion that your puppet is alive, the way it moves should look as natural as the way any other living thing moves. Focusing on subtlety and nuance is the best place to start when learning puppetry. In puppetry, it's always easier to make actions bigger than it is to make them smaller.

The best way to tell if you are over-exaggerating your performance is by recording your performance and watching it back. If there are any aspects that you don't like or are not believable, try changing those things next time you perform. When you watch your next performance, see if the new take is an improvement. Many speakers and comedians develop and perfect their performances this way, and it is perfect for practicing puppetry too.

IF YOU GET FLUSTERED

When performing, there are many things that can distract you from your performance, especially with a live audience or even when on the set of a television puppet show. There can be a lot of pressure or frustration when trying to get a perfect shot. If you happen to get distracted, you need to refocus and maintain control of your hand. Don't get flustered if your lip-sync is off for a moment. Dwelling on these mistakes will only continue to distract you from focusing on your performance. Refocus and keep going.

Now, go ahead and spend some time practicing these techniques using your hand. After you have mastered the techniques in this chapter and they are second nature to you, then you can start breaking the rules to really get the most out of what puppetry has to offer. The possibilities are limitless.

CHAPTER 3 TAKEAWAYS

- Manipulate your puppet with intention.
- When your character talks, make sure to drop the jaw instead of flapping the top of the head.
- Stay in character.

CHAPTER 4
CREATE A COMPELLING CHARACTER

So, let's say you have a puppet. Maybe you gathered the materials, sculpted the foam, and stitched it all by hand. Or, perhaps you purchased a premade puppet, either custom-made or mass-produced from a store. No matter how you procured your puppet, there's only one thing left to do – bring it to life!

In the previous chapter, we learned about the techniques that go into performing and operating your puppet. But even with all of these technical puppeteering skills and a fancy-built puppet, this is not the magic that makes the audience fall in love with your puppet character. It's something else.

For example, Kermit the Frog, though well made, is not an extremely fancy or intricate puppet. There isn't even any foam structure in his head; he is pretty much a sock puppet. And yet the world loves him anyway. This is not just because Jim Henson was good at lip-sync with the puppet's mouth, but because Henson made him into a relatable character that has its own wants, needs, hopes, and dreams.

Now creating a character that an audience can fall in love with is much easier said than done. But, there are some simple steps you can take to start developing a character.

CHECKING OUT CHARACTER

You may not realize this, but you and everyone you know are characters. You've probably heard people described as "a character"; that's just another way of saying they're brimming with personality! In other words, their human qualities are on display. They're funny, happy, sad, excitable, irrational, and generally glued to the roller coaster of life. Think about it: Even when we portray alien or robot characters, we still imbue them with the human experience. Why?

That's what we can relate to. *That's all we know.*

E.T. made us cry without uttering a single word. It wasn't because he was different; it was because he was relatable.

And if you still think such character depth doesn't exist in the world of puppetry, think again. Kermit has pulled generation after generation into his webbed hands by being the everyman. He is the puppet you could pass in the street and maybe even tip your hat to on a good day.

Of course, he's got a lot to take care of—the crazy characters surrounding him, his love and life issues, work, and a whole TV show! So naturally, he gets frustrated and angry and often sits in disbelief. Still, this cloud is lined by laughs, smiles, and endless wisecracks.

He could be any one of us! And that's why he appeals to everyone.

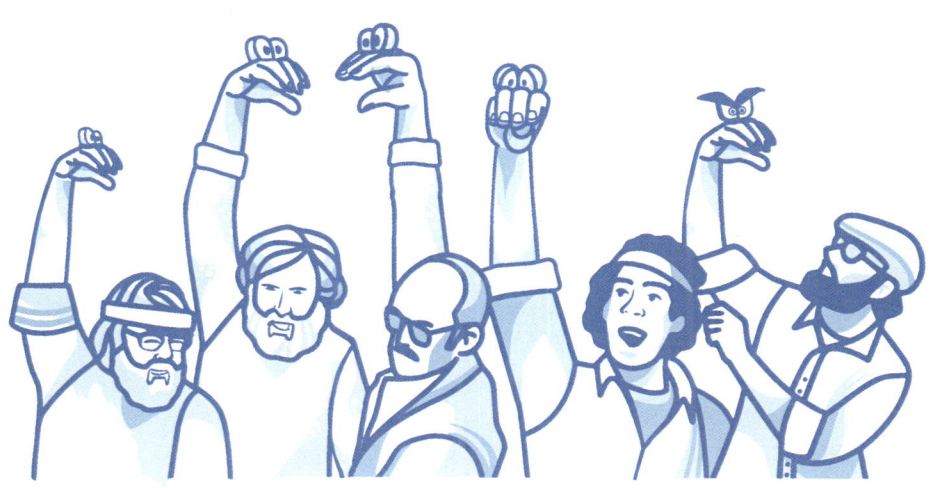

FINDING YOUR PUPPET'S PEOPLE

Characters are designed to relate to a certain group of people. For example, Elmo relates to 3-year-olds. Fozzie Bear relates to people who feel insecure or maybe people who like comedians. These characters are essentially stereotypes designed to appeal to people with specific interests.

However, no one is only one thing. So even though the characters might be stereotypes, they should still be well-rounded. If your puppet character is a chef, they should have a more complex personality beyond simply having a desire to cook. What are their wants and needs? What kind of music do they like? What are other side interests they have? Think of them as real people. For example, I am a school teacher, but that is not the full definition of who I am. We want the personalities of our puppets to be as complex as you or me.

Miss Piggy from the Muppets, for example, is a stereotypical "diva" character. She is outgoing, selfish, and quick to anger. However, she will also have moments where her insecurity shows. These moments make her toughness seem like a way she copes with her anxiety. They make her personality more realistic because she isn't one thing and also isn't perfect, just like people in the real world.

Think of all the personality traits you come across day-to-day and how they're drawn out or hidden at different times. By definition, characters are full of characteristics. They're like a swirling recipe of past, future, and present influences with sprinklings of personality and a dash of psychology. So, really, you can never be too heavy-handed when it comes to fleshing out their character profile. In fact, most puppeteers who create characters claim to fall in love with them throughout the process!

As a character grows and becomes more intricate and human-like before your eyes, you'll naturally feel compelled to keep going. So, let the process flow! Before you know it, you'll have an iconic, relatable, and ground-breaking character on your hands.

WRITE THEIR NARRATIVE

Every good character has a backstory. Whether you choose to share it with your audience or not, it still needs to exist. Think about Big Bird – the large, memorable, yellow-feathered member of *Sesame Street*. While never mentioned outright, we, the viewer, understood that Big Bird was an orphan, taken under the street's figurative wing. How endearing and compelling! So, after deciding who your character is in the first step, it's time to determine how they came to be that way.

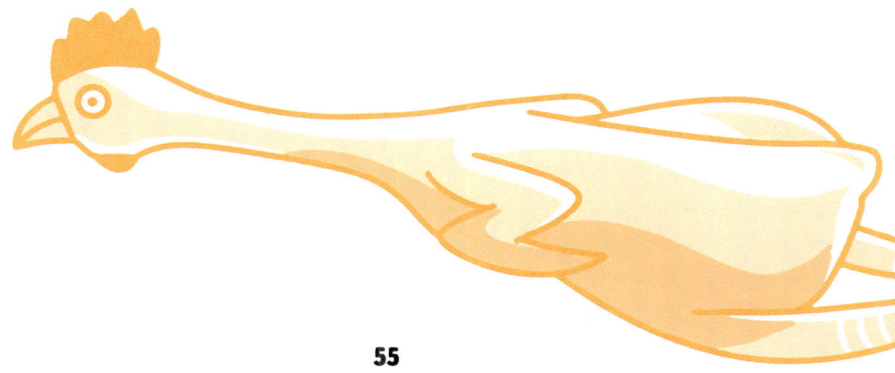

WRITE THEIR NARRATIVE

On *The Muppet Show*, among characters, Kermit's frog status is a given. Yet still, we non-puppets, behind the TV screen, often refer to him by the full title of "Kermit the Frog." And this was no mistake. When Jim Henson first created Kermit, the puppet wasn't even a frog. Jim had not decided to add on the title distinction until a few years later. Though there's no denying the name, Kermit suits his "everyman" persona to a T. His species' ambiguity caused confusion among earlier audiences; it was genius to add "the frog" as a surname.

What I'm trying to say is that names are very, very important. Though a good name cannot cure an unlikeable character, aside from its appearance, the name is the most notable aspect of your character. A name offers a quick glimpse into their personality and makes characters memorable!

So, how do you come up with a name for your puppet?

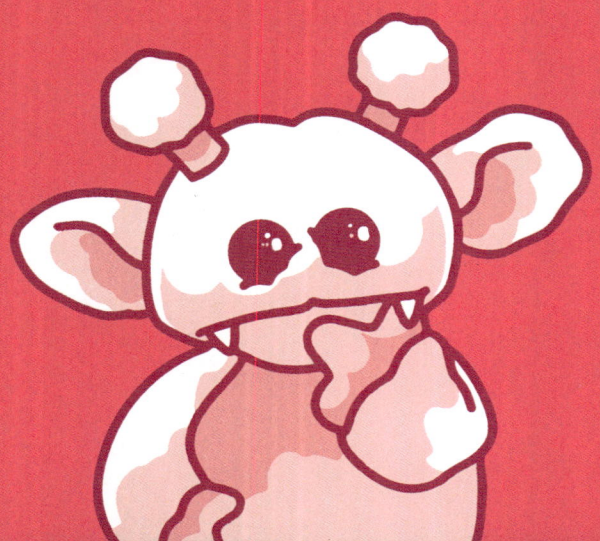

Sometimes inspiration strikes in unlikely places. Growing up, I was fascinated with NASA and outer space. Reading through books, I learned about the Hubble Telescope. It's a telescope that orbits Earth, and since it's high up above the atmosphere, it gives a better view of the universe than telescopes on Earth. It was named after the American astronomer Edwin Hubble. Pretty cool, right? Not only did I think the Hubble Telescope was cool, but I also thought Hubble was a funny word that was fun to say. Years later, when I made an alien puppet, "Hubble the Alien" struck me as the perfect name!

But I'm not always this lucky when coming up with names for my puppets. So here are a few techniques and tools I try when I'm stuck.

- First, I write down any fun names that come to mind on a piece of paper, even if I don't love them.
- Once I'm out of my own ideas, I go to websites for baby names or go through a baby name book for ideas. If I find any that stick out, I add them to the list!
- If I am really stumped, I'll look up some online name generators.
- Double barreling names like Bobby-Joe or Amelia-Rose can be fun too, if I can't decide on one.
- Sometimes I try combining names to create something completely unique, like combining Bobby and Robert to create Bobert!
- Also, will the character need its own version of "The Frog?" Is it "...the Bear", "...the Dolphin" or "...the Zoolag"?

Once I have generated a list, it is much easier to narrow it down until I am left with one!

BODY LANGAUGE

Most of our communication is actually nonverbal. If you don't believe this, try a little experiment next time you meet someone. Stand with your arms crossed, angle yourself away from them, and avoid eye contact. You can lay the charm on thick, but you'll never win them over!

The same goes for your puppet. Do you want them to gesture frantically? Sway calmly? Bop and swoop around like a chilled-out, zen hippie? Or are they a suave city slicker that slinks around and flicks their hair with attitude?

Giving your puppets some of their own unique mannerisms or body movements can create some real, believable moments in your puppetry. It is remarkable how much expression you can achieve with a slight head tilt, a rubbing of the chin, or a head scratch. The physicality of the characters can help draw out their character.

THE VOICE

Your puppet's voice is your next focus. Of course, you'll be the genius behind this voice, so pick something that won't send you running for cough syrup and lozenges afterwards. It's important to generate a sound that you can sustain without pain.

Or, if you'd rather not strain yourself ... go voiceless!

For example, the Muppet scientist Beaker is a character that does not speak. He simply makes a "Meep, Meep!" sound. Of course, even though he does not use words, it is painfully clear what this character is saying and feeling. Another Muppet character, Animal, barely even needs to speak because his prowess on the drums speaks for him. However, he does use frantic body language to hold attention and get his point across. So, you may need to do some hand exercises if you choose this path.

Other than that, you'll have to determine:

- **Pitch** Often a small character will have a higher voice, and the larger the puppet, the deeper the voice. But it could also be funny to do the opposite. And don't forget about volume – is your puppet soft-spoken or a shouter?

- **Dialect** Where is your puppet from? Are they a New Yorker? Do they have a southern drawl?

- **Expression** Some puppets speak in a monotone, while others are highly expressive.

- **Speed** A fast-paced talker may be rushed, scatter-brained, and hard-working. On the other hand, if your puppet is laid-back and easy-going, they may prefer to take their time in speaking.

- **Tone** The attitude of the character toward events and other characters. Are they laid back and agreeable? Do they have a pleasing, helpful, and positive attitude, or are they negative, hopeless, and pessimistic?

You can tweak all of the above to your liking. In that case, the result will almost certainly be an unforgettable and distinct voice that'll carry your puppet through countless shows and performances.

PSYCHOLOGY

Just as every plot needs a driving force, so do the characters. However, don't mistake your puppet's thoughts and philosophy for their narrative. Make sure that the puppet's actions align with their personality and that their motives are clear to the audience. Some puppets are pensive or "zen" and always react measuredly. On the other hand, others are quick to blow a fuse before acting even if nothing happened! Think of what makes you react to certain situations and your thought processes before saying or acting in a specific way. Try to apply them to your puppet, and watch them come to life.

PUPPET WRAP UP

Creating a well-rounded personality for your character is like making a cake. All these elements above – voice, attitude, movements – are ingredients. It takes patience to create a puppet character that can captivate entire audiences and the hearts of the public. However, the power is within your hands – literally and figuratively. So, what are you waiting for? There's a character in everyone!

HOMEWORK!

Write out your character's back story. How old are they? Where do they live? What are their likes and dislikes? What other character traits do they have?

CHAPTER 4 TAKEAWAYS

- The audience falls in love with a relatable character, not a goofy voice or perfect lip-sync.
- Write a backstory for your puppet.
- Let the process of character development flow naturally.

CHAPTER 5
FINDING A STORY

One of the most challenging aspects of making a puppet show is deciding what kind of show you want to do. Are you creating an educational "how-to" show like a cooking show, or a show to teach a talent or skill? Or is it a story with a full narrative? A soap opera? A sitcom? A mystery? Is it a hero's quest to overcome a monster or an everyman's journey from rags to riches?

We are going to explore a couple of these options, the "how-to" and the formal story structure for a show. But let's start with the "how-to" show first. This type of show tends to be a great way to start performing because there is less pressure to create something original.

If I asked you right now to write a full story, you'd probably have to brainstorm some ideas for a while. However, if I asked you to write a show that explains how to tie your shoes or make a peanut butter and jelly sandwich, that would be much easier, and you could get started right away.

"How-to" instructions also provide a good structure for creating some funny situations or fanciful premises. For example, instead of showing how to make something ordinary like a peanut butter and jelly sandwich, you can show how to make a Unicorn Treat. What would be the steps to make a Unicorn Treat? Maybe rainbow sherbet, mixed with rainbow sprinkles, and some pink cotton candy on top. All of a sudden, we have a whimsical show that could inspire more stories.

Here is an example of a basic outline.

HOW TO MAKE A PEANUT BUTTER & JELLY SANDWICH

FIRST
Pull out two slices of bread and open the jars of peanut butter and jelly.

NEXT
Spread the peanut butter onto one slice of bread.

THEN
Spread jelly on the other slice of bread.

AFTER THAT
Lay the two slices on top of each other.

FINALLY
Take a big bite out of your peanut butter and jelly sandwich and ENJOY!

HOW TO CATCH A MAGIC UNICORN

FIRST Gather the ingredients to make their favorite treats: rainbow sherbet mixed with rainbow sprinkles and pink cotton candy.

NEXT Mix it all together in a big bowl and stir it 7 times, no more, no less, because 7 is the unicorn's favorite number.

THEN Bake them, but not in an oven – right in the sun!

AFTER THAT Lay out the colorful treats in a pile and stack them as high as you can.

FINALLY The unicorns will come stampeding in! Duck! Take cover! Watch your head!! RUNNNNNNN!

NOW YOU TRY EXPLAINING SOMETHING!

. . . .

FIRST

. . . .

NEXT

. . . .

THEN

. . . .

AFTER THAT

. . . .

FINALLY

Once you have these steps filled out, most of the work is done. If you use this "how-to" form as a script for your puppet to perform—and you have a well-developed puppet character—then you have the makings of a show of your very own. With the lessons we learned in *Chapter 4: Create a Compelling Character*, it's mostly a matter of understanding how your character would react to these steps. Take the unicorn treat example. How would your character feel about unicorns? Would they like them? Maybe your character LOVES unicorns, but is allergic to them! Details like this inherently create some funny tension.

FINDING A SHOW – TAKEAWAYS

- If you don't have an idea for a story, start with what you know. Have your puppet teach a skill step by step.

- Follow a simple "how to" structure.

- Use your imagination to create something magical or fanciful your puppet can make step by step.

FORMAL STORY STRUCTURE

Without a properly structured story, your puppets are just talking heads on stage with no connection to the action that happens around them. Every great puppet show starts with a phenomenal storyline that pushes the plot ahead. Coming up with a story means creating characters, history, conflict, and more. Even though writing a puppet show can feel like a lot of work, when broken down, it is pretty simple.

STARTING WITH THE PLOT

To avoid feeling overwhelmed when you sit down to write your story, start by following the basic story arc that all famous tales stem from – an event changes the main character. At the beginning of the story, the main character starts out one way, and they are changed by the end. The situations, events, and conflicts that change the character make the story.

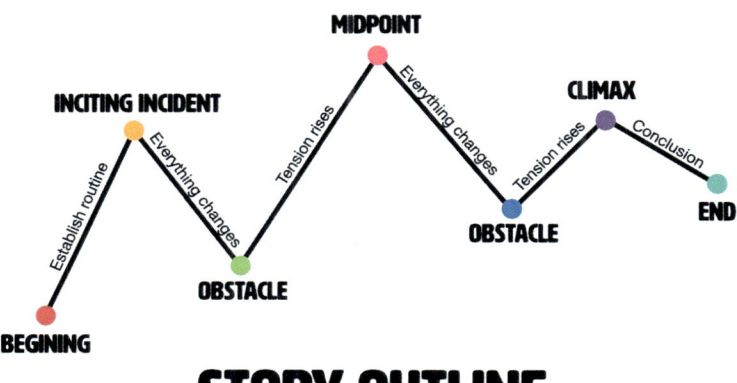

STORY OUTLINE
WRITING A PUPPET SHOW

BEGINNING

Your story should start by establishing the routine of your characters. This is the exposition. What is a normal day like for them? What is their history or "backstory"? Lay all of this out in the first few minutes of your show. All kinds of stories, from Hollywood blockbusters to fairytales to ancient myths, provide some form of exposition, introducing the audience to the character, setting, and in some cases even the conflict, all within the first few minutes. Think about Little Red Riding Hood. From the very first words of the story, we learn that she's a girl in a village by the woods, and that she always wears a recognizable red hood.

INCITING INCIDENT

After establishing your characters' routines and setting up the exposition, you hit the first plot point – an inciting incident that throws off the character's usual routine. This part in the story is where everything changes, and the action of the story begins. In Little Red Riding Hood, Red's mother tells her that her grandma is sick and she must deliver a basket to her. This is the *inciting incident* – the task sets the story in motion.

OBSTACLES & RISING ACTION

From the inciting incident, everything in the story is flipped on its head: routines change, people are exposed, and everything is different from what was originally set up in the exposition. This series of obstacles is the *rising action* that leads us to the eventual climax. In Little Red, the tension rises and builds when Red disobeys her mother's warning to stay on the path. This choice sets her up for the encounter with the wolf.

MIDPOINT

Within this rising action, you'll also have a *midpoint*. This midpoint gives the audience a bit of rest from the obstacles and offers some hope, though uncertainty and even fear may remain. For Little Red Riding Hood, this is her eventual arrival at her grandma's house. However, the story is not done yet!

CLIMAX

After a few more obstacles, the story reaches the *climax* – the peak that the arc had pointed to from the beginning. In Little Red Riding Hood, this would be when Red confronts the wolf, dressed up as her grandma; it ends after the wolf has eaten Red.

END

The conclusion is the *falling action* of the story, leading all the way to the resolution that wraps the story up with a nice bow and signals the ending of the narrative. Here, the audience and the main character have to ask themselves, how will the protagonist escape the situation?

The resolution can be achieved in many ways, but is rarely neutral – it almost always leads to either a sad or a happy ending. (Some stories, especially fairytales, have multiple versions of the resolution. For instance, in some versions of Little Red Riding Hood, a lumberjack breaks in and stops the wolf immediately and frees Red and the grandma. In other versions, the lumberjack puts stones in the Wolf's belly to slow him down and eventually stop him, but does not save the grandma.)

This part is also where you can wrap up any moral or message you are trying to get across to the audience, if you have one. It is best to do this subtly, though; making the message too obvious can make the story seem boring or predictable.

BASIC PLOTS

Follow the story arc, and your puppet shows will have just the right number of twists and turns to keep your audience engaged. There are basic plot lines and genres that have been used since the ancient Greeks to keep a story on the move. These are great to keep in mind when crafting a great story.

- **Comedy** Comedy can be broken into a ton of subgenres, but it's basically a series of chaotic events that lead to a resolution.
- **Tragedy** On the other side, tragedy is all about the character's flaws and how they are negatively affected by the mistakes they make.
- **Good Beats Evil** The main character sets out to defeat an evil force that threatens them or their community. This plot is also known as "Overcoming the Monster" though the problem doesn't have to be a literal "monster"; it can be a disaster or some other event.
- **Rags to Riches** This situation often portrays a person's rise from poverty to wealth, or from regular life to the heights of fame.
- **The Important Quest** This plot tells about one character or a group of characters who embark on a mission.

- **Homeward Bound** This story describes a person who has left their hometown, had some adventures, and now is returning.
- **Rebirth** These stories end with a clear, new perspective and change in the character's life. These often include coming-of-age stories.

INVEST IN YOUR CHARACTERS

The plot can be amazingly crafted, but without well-rounded characters, the story will have no heart to it. Here are five characters you should have in your story. They should be fully developed using the methods we covered in *Chapter 4: Create a Compelling Character*.

- **Protagonist** is your main character, the most relatable character that we follow in the story. Your audience needs someone to root for, and the protagonist is that character.
- **Antagonist** is the character who resists the protagonist. Your audience also needs someone to root against; in comes the antagonist.
- **Sidekick** is the protagonist's helper. They often offer comedic relief by contrasting with their heroic counterpart.
- **Mentor** guides the protagonist along their journey and helps the story maintain traction. They give advice and keep the protagonist focused on the end goal.
- **Love Interest** is a great character for giving the audience a deeper look into your protagonist's feelings and inner life.

KEEP BUILDING

The story arc, basic plot lines, and essential characters present in your story all help you produce a workable product. Keep these tips in mind when crafting your next puppet show.

CHAPTER 5 TAKEAWAYS

- Following a story arc is a great way to develop a show that feels complete.
- Know what kind of story you are trying to tell.
- If you are having trouble getting your story started, try writing the end first, then working backwards.

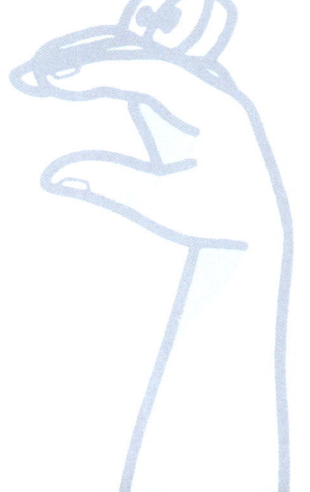

CHAPTER 6
THE INS & OUTS OF TELEVISION PUPPETRY

Jim Henson, the creator of the Muppets, said that "simple is good." He kept this energy when it came to filming his shows, a legacy that continues today. With Henson's monitor-style of shooting, few tools are needed to create a captivating performance. He helped to prove that with a few simple techniques, anyone can excel as a puppeteer.

Live stage performance methods don't all translate well to the screen when it comes to puppetry, though. There are different styles, tips, and tools you need to think about and use when performing for television. Knowing the difference and understanding how and why we use a monitor for filming puppets for the screen is vital in creating a realistic puppet show.

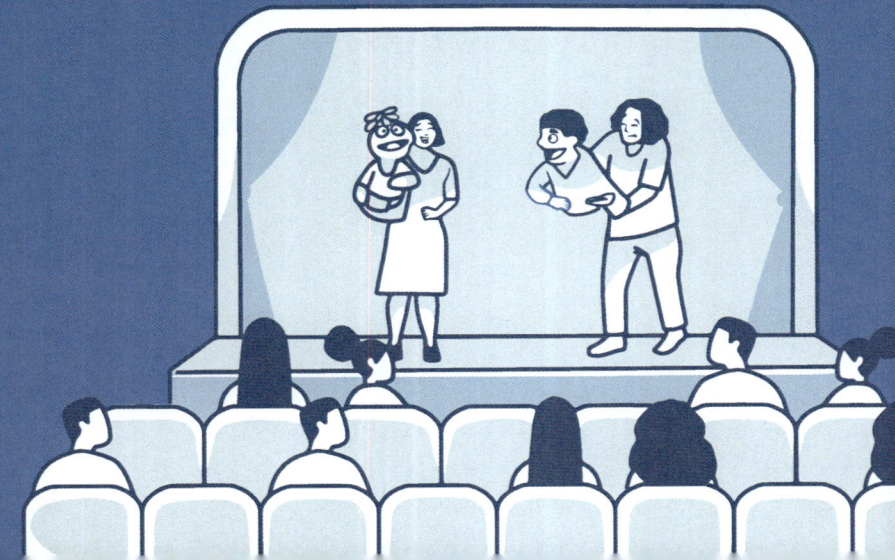

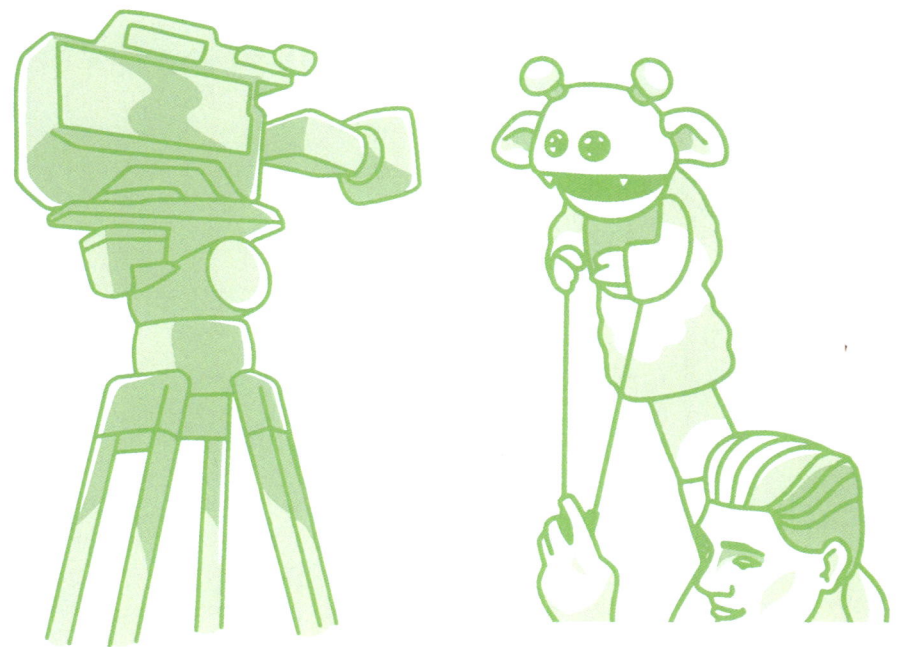

HOW TO PERFORM FOR THE SCREEN

A puppeteer performing on stage needs to act through not only the puppet but with their whole body. Generally, their goal is to keep the audience's focus on the puppet, so it is important for them to move their body in a way that either doesn't draw attention away from the puppet or somehow mirrors the energy of the puppet. The puppeteer may even wear all black to blend in with the background, so their presence doesn't throw off the show. In addition, in a stage setting, each person in the audience has their own vantage point. In other words, every person sees a slightly different show since they each observe it from a different angle. This makes it impossible for a puppet on stage to feel like they are directly talking to each audience member at one time. In this situation, the puppet can't and won't make eye contact with everyone in the audience, and that's okay.

The exact opposite happens with performances on screen. Even if multiple people are viewing the same screen, it feels like the puppet is talking directly to them if the puppeteer is using perfect eye focus and making their puppet look into the lens of the camera. Also, in the video, the puppeteer is not seen by the audience. The top of the puppeteer's head or even an inch of their forearm showing can spoil the entire illusion of the puppet show. To avoid this situation, puppeteers for television use a monitor.

Television puppeteers look at a monitor to ensure that the actions of the puppet are displayed correctly. In addition, looking at the monitor allows the performer, in real-time to see what the viewer will see on TV. This way, they can adjust their performance to connect better through the screen. (In contrast, the puppeteers at a live stage show typically look at the puppet.)

There are a few things a puppeteer looks for while watching their puppet on a monitor. The first is good eye focus. As mentioned before, the puppet has to be able to look straight into the camera in order to effectively connect with the viewer at home. Filmed shows don't have the luxury of being in the same time and space as the audience, so they use this technique to create a sense of intimate connection. Also, the puppeteer can clearly see how their puppet fits in the shot and whether their lip-sync matches the intensity they want. The puppeteer can use the monitor to check that the puppet is naturally walking into the frame without their arm creeping into view. Lastly, the puppeteer can refer to the monitor when performing tasks on the screen. So whether your puppet is making a sandwich or banging on the drums, you have a perfect view of your performance if you are using a monitor.

The technique of using a monitor to see your puppeteering in real-time has been around for a long time and was popularized by the work of Jim Henson. It is the primary method used by puppeteers in the industry and is regarded as essential for anyone who wants to make a filmed puppet show.

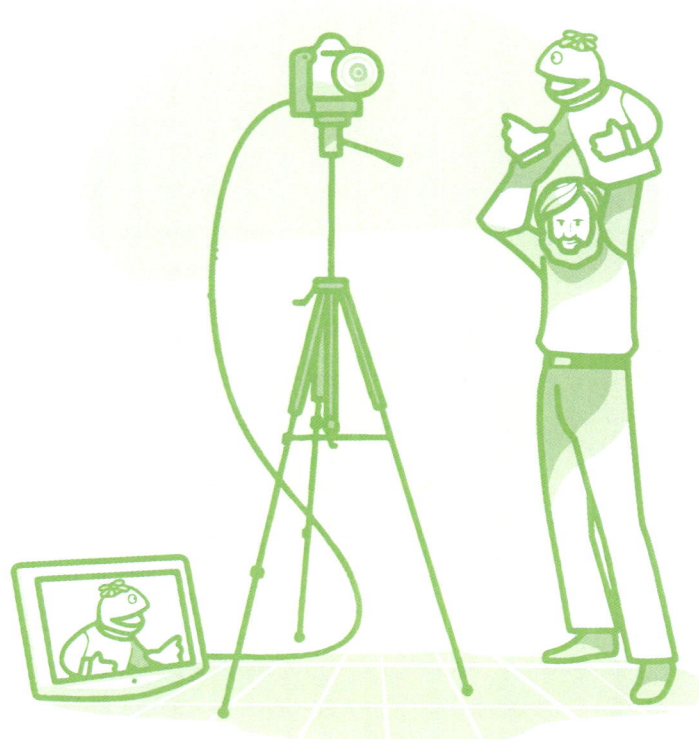

THE HENSON METHOD OF PUPPETEERING

Jim Henson not only created the monitor method to record his puppet shows for television but also the raised set so the puppeteers don't need to scrunch down in uncomfortable positions that make it difficult to perform. Filmed puppet sets are typically raised five feet above ground, allowing the puppeteers to have a full range of motion without worrying about inching into the shot. Since the set is so high up, the puppeteers tended to be tall. The raised nature of the camera and set meant that anyone lacking the necessary height had to wear platform shoes or stand on an elevated surface.

The monitor and the script are located slightly below the puppeteers' eye level. This way, the puppeteers don't have to look up at their puppet when performing, and they can get a clearer view of the crucial performance aspects we mentioned, like making sure the puppet is making eye contact with the camera.

The Henson method of puppeteering also considers different positioning of a character – the "downstage" and "upstage" of the screen. Downstage is when the puppet is close to the camera. This positioning is the most commonly used at the start of the scene. Later, the characters often move back to reveal more of the scenery and world. Upstage refers to characters far away from the camera. A popular technique used by Henson to create laughter was to use a puppet to flail around upstage to distract from the puppet grabbing attention downstage.

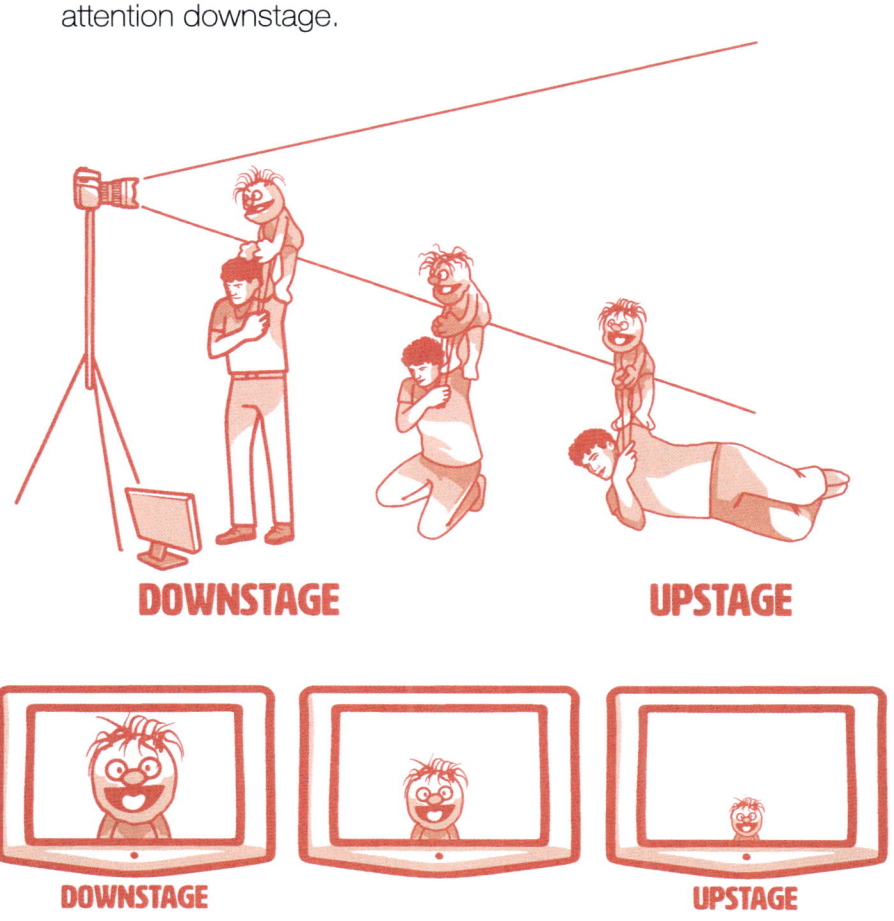

DOWNSTAGE   **UPSTAGE**

DOWNSTAGE   **UPSTAGE**

The monitor is necessary to make these little techniques work. Without the monitor, it's hard to position the puppet just right while keeping the puppeteer out of view. The monitor technique is here to stay, and for a good reason, so puppeteers need to adapt.

TOOLS FOR THE MONITOR TECHNIQUE

The great thing about monitor puppetry is that it's easy to accomplish. First, you need a camera. That can mean pretty much any smartphone in today's world, but keep in mind that you do need a way to hook it up to the monitor. Next, you need a tripod. As mentioned before, ideally, the set for your show will be raised up about five feet high. Using a tripod, you can position the camera at the level where it needs to be. Lastly, you need a small television or computer monitor. Most modern cameras have no problem hooking up to a TV or computer monitor with a USB, HDMI, or D-Port connection.

Years ago, a monitor would have been expensive and tricky to find. Luckily, now monitors are relatively cheap and easy to come across. You can find an inexpensive TV or computer monitor to use online or even at a thrift store. You might even find one for free if you ask around.

In a pinch, you can use an iPad or tablet as a monitor. Simply hook up your device to the camera, and you're good to go. These options make producing a good-quality puppet show without a professional set or budget more accessible than ever before.

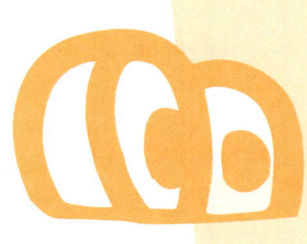

PRO TIP!
I have recommendations for different monitors and tips on how to connect your phone or camera to a monitor on my website. For the most up-to-date list, visit www.PuppetNerd.com

Though it's best to raise up your set just like the professionals, if this is difficult for you to do, you can lay on the floor to keep yourself out of view. This limits your range of movement and can get uncomfortable quickly, but it's a reminder that there's always a way to fulfill your puppeteering dreams.

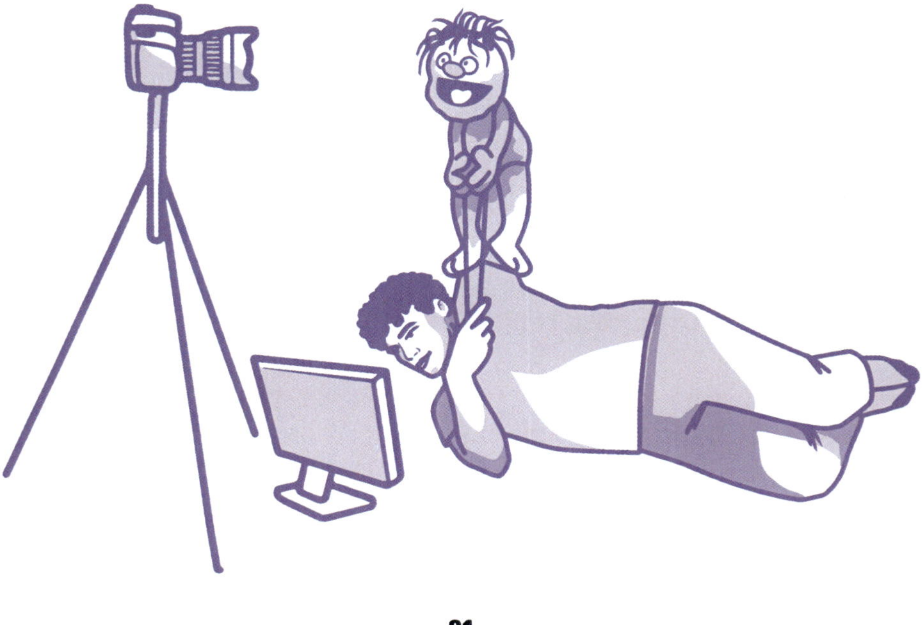

TIPS FOR A SUCCESSFUL FILMED PUPPET SHOW

There are several tips and tricks you can use to make a successful filmed puppet show. The first hurdle the puppeteer must pass is getting used to being down below and having the camera positioned up high. This can be challenging to get used to, but soon you get the hang of concentrating on the monitor, and the puppet follows suit.

It's important to note that the image on the monitor will not be a perfect mirror image of what is being performed. Instead, this image is the inverse of what you're doing. If your hand is facing left, the monitor will show it facing right. This can be tricky to get the hang of, so plenty of practice will help. When performing, it's essential to look at the monitor to see what the viewer sees and align your puppet accordingly.

An excellent exercise you can do to get used to the camera's frame, and the puppet's positioning within it, is to make the puppet look at all four corners of the camera. This fast exercise can help orient you in the frame and make sure you have a nice range of motion moving forward. Also, when you're first beginning to puppeteer on screen, you can practice by having your puppet lip-sync to a song that you know well. This way, you can focus on the puppet's actions and movements without worrying about your lines and how you are delivering them. Focus on the basics before you move to the advanced techniques.

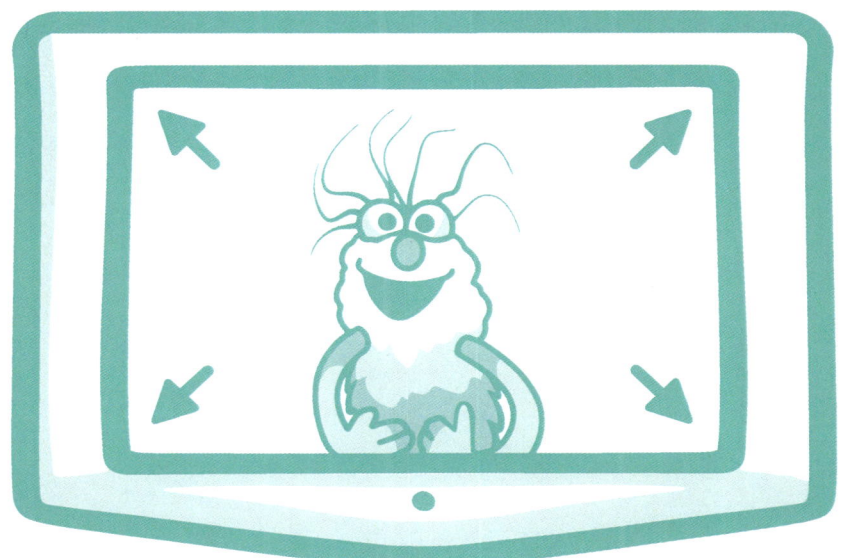

When you've got the basic techniques down, you can relax a bit more. A professional puppeteer isn't thinking about their puppet and their hand in it all the time. Skilled puppeteering becomes similar to walking. Your movements become automatic, and you trust that you can move correctly without having to constantly check everything. The monitor is just there to help you double-check, regroup, and stay in frame.

Puppeteering on screen is all about creating an accurate illusion. This is why you see puppets come from the left or right of the screen, but generally not the top or bottom. In real life, someone wouldn't exit the stage by disappearing into the abyss below, so your puppet shouldn't either as this would break the illusion of "Ground" we discussed earlier. Puppeteering is also like regular acting; the puppet will naturally adopt the character you have as you control it.

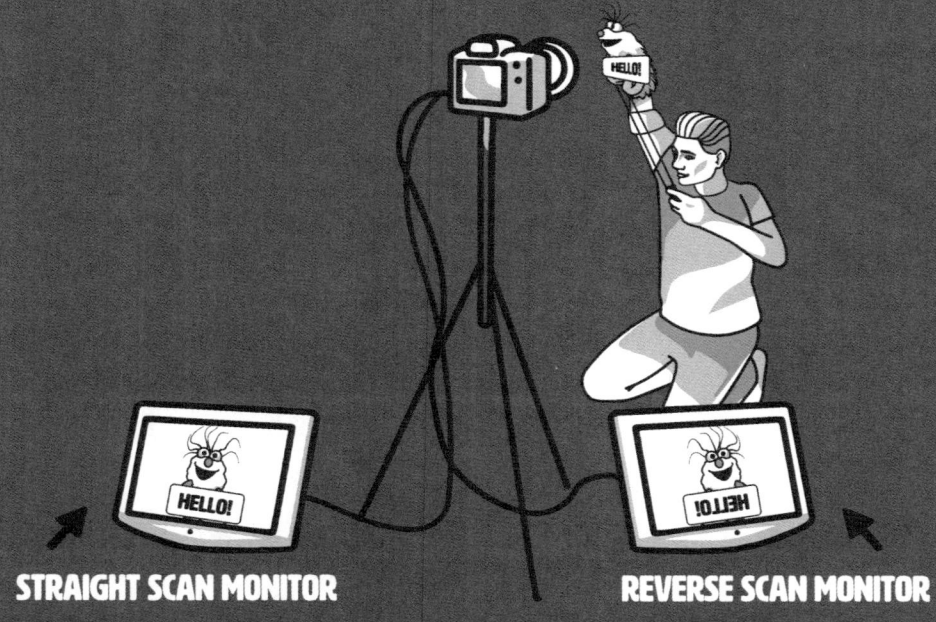

STRAIGHT SCAN MONITOR

REVERSE SCAN MONITOR

TYPES OF MONITORS

There are two types of monitors. The more common type is the straight scan monitor. This is the type of monitor we've been discussing throughout the book. It's widely available and popular with both professional and amateur puppeteers alike.

With a straight scan monitor, your movements look reversed. Most puppeteers prefer this monitor because the viewer will see exactly what appears on the monitor. Thus, the performer can easily rely on the monitor alone to capture the correct movements for their puppets and give a more believable performance. Big shows like *The Muppet Show*, *Bear in the Big Blue House*, and *Fraggle Rock* have all used straight scan monitors.

The next type of monitor used in puppetry on film is a reverse scan. This monitor provides a mirror image of what you're doing, like the front-facing camera on your phone. The image is similar to what you get from a mirror. You might think this monitor would be easier for the puppeteer because they don't have to do the opposite of what they're thinking to make the same image. However, because the image they are looking at isn't made for TV, they miss out on many details, especially when using letters or numbers. With this type of monitor, words will appear backwards on the screen.

GET IN THE SHOT

As mentioned before, when puppetry is performed on stage, the audience has the ability to look anywhere they want. But this is not true in film. When recording a show with a camera you have full control over what the audience sees. As a result, you can show the audience only what they need to see, which helps you in telling a story.

It's helpful to understand how a camera actually "sees." The lens of a camera is relatively small even though it is able to see things that are quite large. And the further back you put the camera, the more of the room it picks up.

By positioning a camera at the proper distance and height for your set, you'll find a "sweet spot" where you can perform without getting in the shot. However, you might notice a small problem if your puppet needs to move upstage (further away from the camera).

The further back you
go with your puppet,
the wider the field of
vision is for the
camera. So, you
may suddenly find
yourself in the shot.

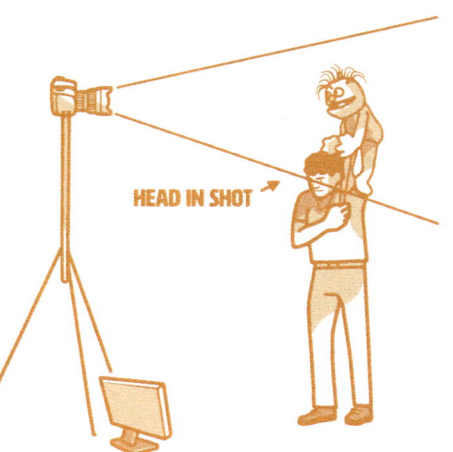

To solve this problem, you can either raise the camera
higher or angle it slightly up. Angling the camera up will
give you much more space to exist as a puppeteer
while you move your puppet upstage.

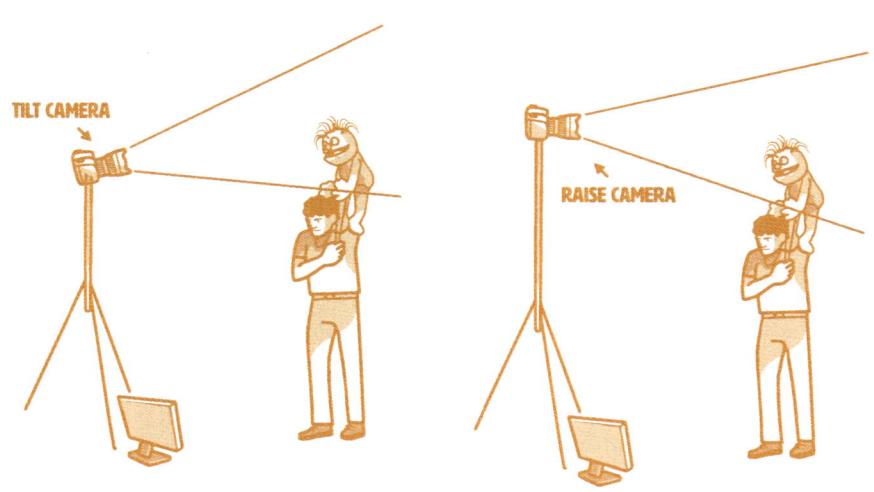

However, although angling the camera is the most ideal solution from a performing standpoint, it isn't always possible if there is a particular background or set piece you need in the shot. You might need to sew yourself into a couch or cut a hole in a table instead.

Before filming your real take, you will want to film a test shot. Go through all the motions you plan to do with your puppet character to see if you need to adjust the position of your camera.

CHAPTER 6 TAKEAWAYS

- Using a monitor is not a luxury for television puppetry; it's a **necessity** and the only way you will be able to give a believable performance.

- A straight scan monitor gives you a true image of what the audience will see.

- The more you use a monitor, the more comfortable you will be.

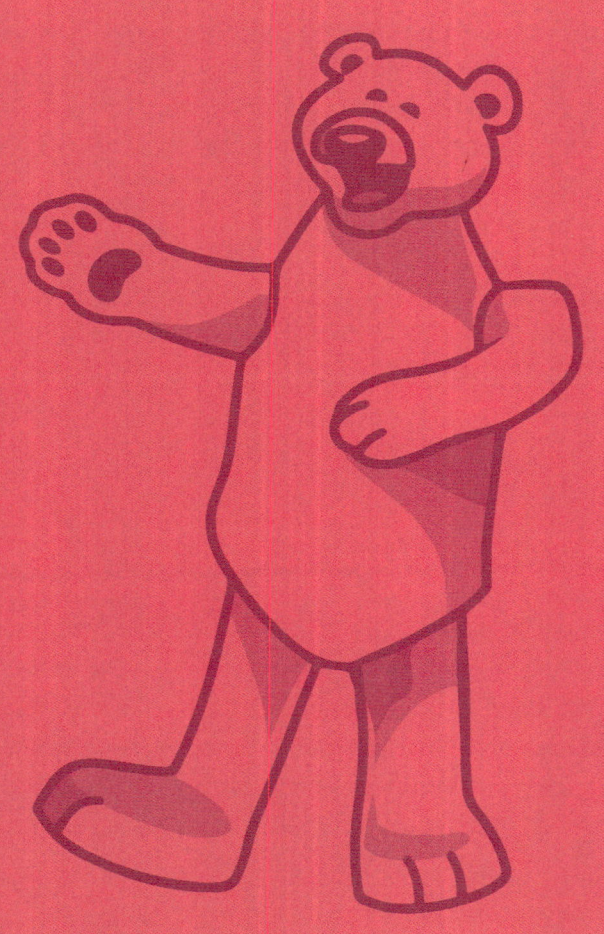

CHAPTER 7
BUILDING THE SHOW!

So let's say you've already written your story and script – congrats! What you have is the DNA of your puppet show. Creating a puppet is where the fun really begins. Let's get to it!

CHARACTER DESIGN

It's likely that after writing your story, you already have a few faces, shapes, colors, and fuzzy silhouettes swirling around your mind. Details of how a character looks sometimes become part of the dialogue or plot points, and is occasionally even the driving force in the story. Think of the story "Chicken Little." Even the title has major character design elements built right into it. If your show has no specific references to how the characters look, then you have a lot of design freedom.

But let's say you want a completely original design – here's your crash course checklist:

- **Shapes and proportions** Big, round head with a little body? Tall and skinny with a little square face? The proportions of your character can dictate how they're perceived by the audience, e.g., comedically proportioned or human-like.

- **Color** Color can be an important tool for character design. If I mentioned a red monster on *Sesame Street*… you immediately know exactly who I am talking about without even hearing the name. Color is what people generally remember, even if they can't remember much else. You can even use it to inform the audience about the temperament of the character. Maybe the blue character is sad, and the red character is angry. This is not a hard and fast rule, but it's a fun idea to play with.

- **Species** Human, animal, beast, or blob – whatever you're feeling! Maybe you intended for your puppets to be humanoid characters, but I challenge you to experiment and imagine other concepts, too. It could really make your story more interesting or playful. For example, let's look at *Hamlet* by William Shakespeare.

Hamlet is set in Elsinore, a remote royal castle in Denmark. But what if instead we placed it in Africa? And instead of human characters, let's change all the characters to lions. Does this story sound familiar? This is exactly what Disney did to create *The Lion King*, and it worked out pretty well for them.

- **Clothing** It's not a necessity. Most of my puppets, for instance, do not have clothes. But it could be a fun design choice that can inform the audience, especially if your character has a certain profession, like a dentist or a firefighter. Clothes can add a distinct touch, convey backstory, and more.

HOW TO MAKE A PUPPET

A quick secret: Making puppets doesn't have to be complicated. Remember that a green coat with ping pong balls apparently can get you pretty far. So, you don't need to be a professional at sewing or anything like that. Just have faith in yourself and a hefty dose of patience. It won't be easy the first time around, and   you will make mistakes, but all that does is add an exciting backstory and charm to your creation!

PRO TIP!
We have free puppet patterns, step-by-step instructions, and tutorials listed on the resources page at the end of the book! Check it out!

HOW TO MAKE A PUPPET

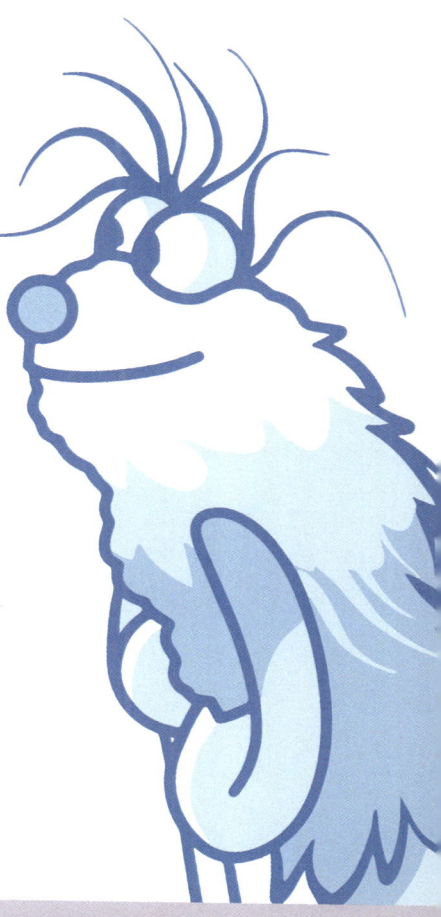

Gather the necessary tools and materials: scissors, sewing needle, thread, felt or fur. And follow along with some of our tutorials and patterns.

Visit SnoofsOfTheWorld.com to download the easy-to-assemble Snoof Puppet Pattern. Following this template and instructions, you could make a simple puppet in under an hour. You'll find many more step-by-step guides that'll help you to create your ideal puppet at PuppetNerd.com.

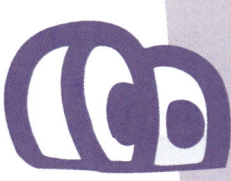

PRO TIP!

A fun detail for your puppet is to add a material that adds "secondary movement." By adding wispy light materials to your puppet, such as long thin fur or faux feathers, you can achieve movement that is generated as a reaction to the primary motions made by a character.

DIY PUPPET SETS

The sets for your show can be as simple or complicated as you want. You could even use a regular room in your house, furniture and all. Sometimes, nature has already given you everything you need, too. If you have an outdoor setting in mind, all you have to do is open the door and go outside! Really, the world is your puppet stage – make good use of it! But if your show has more of a fantasy style, you will of course have to custom-make something.

One way to create a set you need is to have a *backdrop* – a painted piece of fabric hung in the background. You can paint whatever scene you want on it. Muslin is a great fabric to use as it is cheap, lightweight, and takes paint well. And as a bonus, it is easy to roll up for storage. However, you might end up needing something a little sturdier that won't wrinkle and has the benefit of being able to attach props to it, such as a picture frame or other fixtures. For that, I would recommend making flats out of thin plywood or cardboard.

GREEN SCREEN

Another option for a backdrop is a *green screen* that lets you choose whatever background you want and even swap backgrounds instantly, too, using a computer. It's an excellent investment and supplies endless customizability, fun, and easy control over how you tell your story. A green screen is a solid-colored background (usually green though sometimes blue) which allows you to easily replace the background with any image or video of your choice. Many craft stores offer large rolls of solid green and blue fabric that can be cut to form a makeshift green screen. Next, all you need is a camera and good video editing software to chroma key out the background. First, you video record your puppet against a solid-color background, typically green or blue, and then use chroma keying – a technique of composing two video files together. In other words, you remove that green or blue background in video editing software and add a new one, making your puppet look like it's in outer space, underwater, in a rainforest, or anywhere you can imagine.

With a green screen, there is no limit to what your setting can be. You could use video backgrounds and photos as backgrounds. You could even draw your own! If you want to get started right now, we have some background images on our resource page that you can use right away!

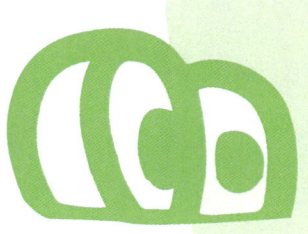

PRO TIP!
We have free backgrounds to use with a green screen at ThePuppetClub.com! Check it out!

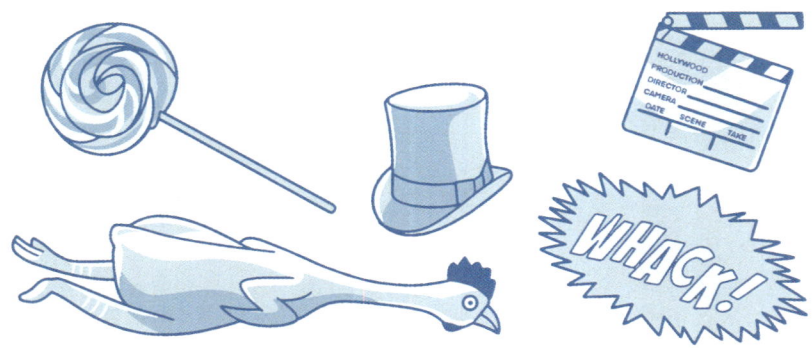

PROPS

While it's true puppets aren't exactly known for their ability to pick things up with ease, some plots call for props. What's more, props add a particularly immersive property to some scenes; it's always interesting to see characters interact with their surroundings. To keep things light and easy to work with, I recommend sketching the props on cardboard and then cutting them out and decorating them however you wish. But don't hesitate to nose about and get creative. For example, dollhouse furniture is ideal for beds or dining tables. Or, take a page out of the Punch & Judy playbook to source props that'll make a lot of funny, whacky noises! Nothing quite compares to the sound of one puppet whacking an empty plastic bottle over another puppet's head. In short – get creative!

SUPPORTING CHARACTERS

Don't forget about the other characters in the scene with your protagonist. Even if you are the only performer, a show with a few characters can still be doable. For example, you could perform a show with a different puppet on each hand. Another option, if you are skilled with video editing, is using a split-screen, which allows you to film your characters separately and then digitally place both of them in the same scene. It can be tricky to line up the timing, but with a little practice, it can work well.

Although you can use these techniques to put up a show with two or more characters, it isn't always recommended. Unless you plan on growing a few extra arms, if your story requires multiple characters, you might want to hire some roles out. Be it friends, family, or anyone else you can get to help with your show – why not ask them to join the fun?

And there you have it! What are you waiting for? It's time to load your characters into the wagon and get your puppet show on the road!

CHAPTER 7 TAKEAWAYS

- Try to keep a consistent style and aesthetic with the design of your show.
- Design elements can enhance the story you are telling.
- You can get your story out quickly by using existing spaces by filming outside or in your own home. Simple is good.

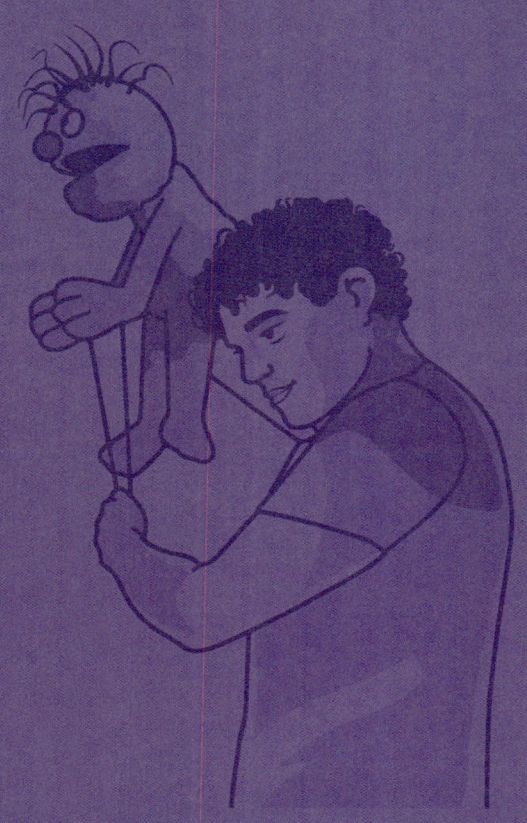

CHAPTER 8
PRACTICE

We've heard it all before: "Practice makes perfect" and "A journey of a thousand miles begins with a single step." But do these sayings actually hold any truth? **Yes**. Now we're going to dive deeper and discover why practicing really matters, and learn about the best way to practice and rehearse with your puppets.

WHY DO WE AVOID PRACTICE?

In its simplest form, practice is repeating something until you get better at it. Then, once you get better, you practice more, and you get even better again – rinse and repeat! So, if it's really that easy, why does it seem impossible at times? Why does practice sometimes give you a headache or feel like a chore?

First, practice is actively admitting you're kind of wrong over and over again until you get it right. No one likes admitting their mistakes or imperfections.

Second, practice requires stomaching multiple failures before success. And failures do not feel nice.

Third, it can be hard to watch those who've already perfected what we're still practicing. But here's a secret. Even the most skilled puppeteers have almost certainly considered throwing their puppet out the window multiple times before. And behind every masterpiece is a trash can full of crumpled paper. While avoiding practice helped no one, perseverance has led to some wonderful puppetry shows. And that is why it's so important to practice.

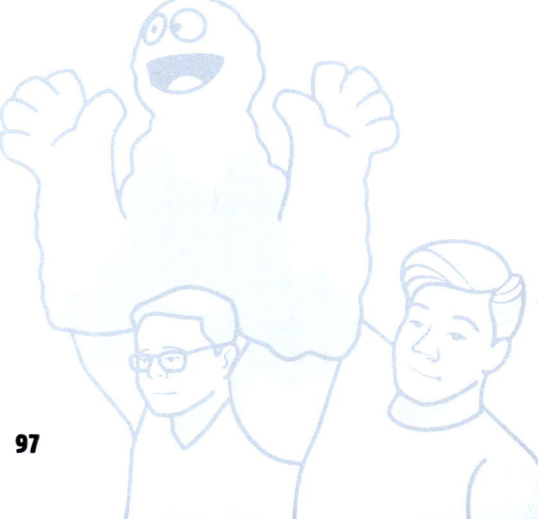

SHOULD YOU BE PRACTICING PUPPETRY NOW?

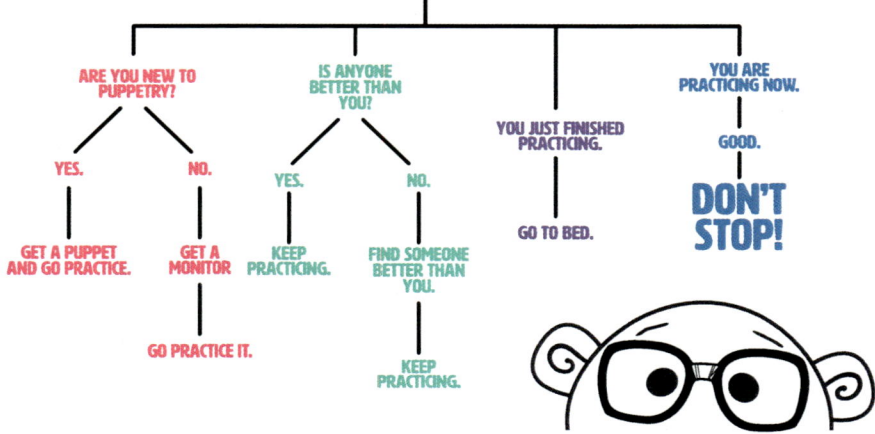

ARE YOU NEW TO PUPPETRY?
- YES. → GET A PUPPET AND GO PRACTICE.
- NO. → GET A MONITOR → GO PRACTICE IT.

IS ANYONE BETTER THAN YOU?
- YES. → KEEP PRACTICING.
- NO. → FIND SOMEONE BETTER THAN YOU. → KEEP PRACTICING.

YOU JUST FINISHED PRACTICING.
GO TO BED.

YOU ARE PRACTICING NOW.
GOOD.
DON'T STOP!

HOW TO PRACTICE EFFECTIVELY

The key to greatness has been and always will be knowing how to practice and then doing it.

SET GOALS

The thing about dreams is that they're hard to remember day-to-day. So when the final destination seems impossibly far away, "what's for dinner" always seems more pressing. And that's why you need reminders.

First: Determine your goal. Maybe the goal is to become really good at manipulating two arm rods at the same time. Or getting to a point where creating the illusion of ground for your puppet is second nature. Choose one goal at a time to focus on when you are getting started.

Next: Find a person who's already there – in other words, a role model. If you know them in person, great! If not, that's fine, too. If you can find a figure to look up to, research how much work and dedication it took them to get where they are. This information can help you to keep things real. Whether it's Jim Henson or other puppeteers from history, being able to watch and study people who have mastered the techniques is extremely helpful. There are many resources you will be able to find to help you do this.

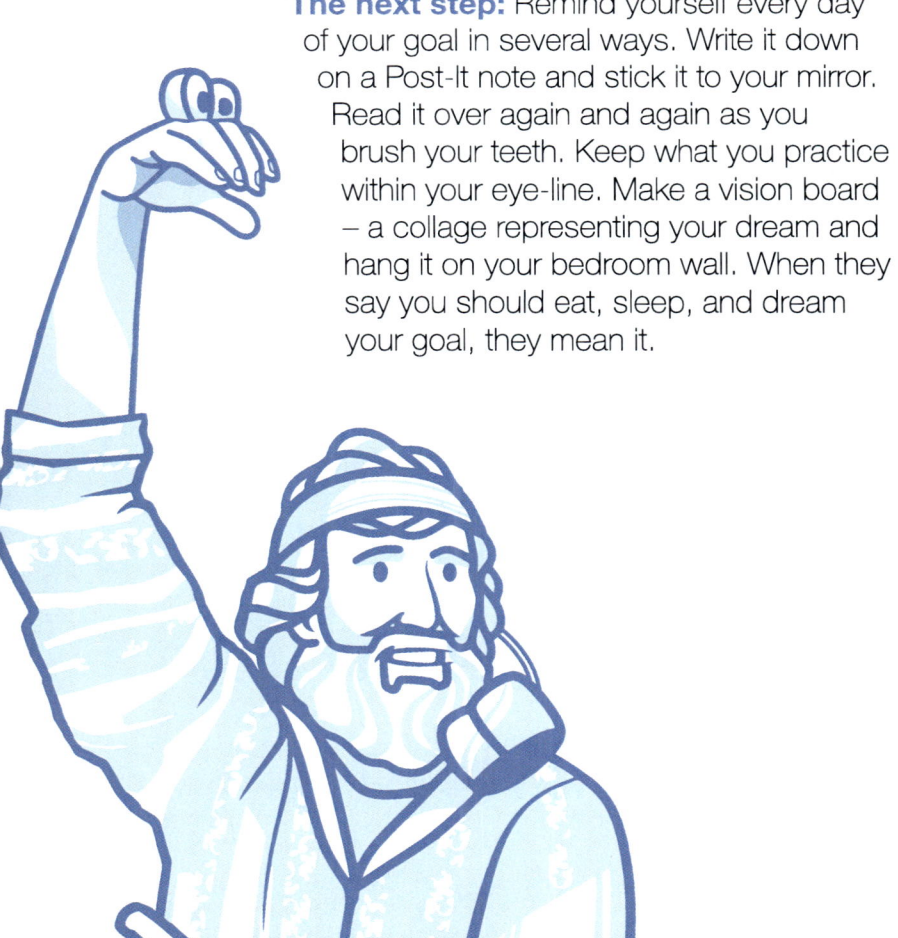

The next step: Remind yourself every day of your goal in several ways. Write it down on a Post-It note and stick it to your mirror. Read it over again and again as you brush your teeth. Keep what you practice within your eye-line. Make a vision board – a collage representing your dream and hang it on your bedroom wall. When they say you should eat, sleep, and dream your goal, they mean it.

ROUTINE

Routines are extremely effective when it comes to boosting our confidence and keeping motivation levels high. But, of course, these also just happen to be the perfect recipe for practice sessions. So, get time on your side and create a schedule for your practice. Make a clear layout of how you plan to spend your time. For example, you might practice for half an hour to unwind after school or work and then an hour again later in the evening. Reassess and prioritize your time. Are you spending too long scrolling through social media online when you could be practicing your puppeteering techniques? Do you learn best in the morning, evening, or night? Also, remember to schedule some break time into your week and allow for little rewards along the way!

To fit practice into your schedule and also have a productive rehearsal, you can follow a "practicing cold" technique. This technique means practicing a specific skill in one take. When I worked as a magician, I learned that it's best not to practice the same trick multiple times in a row because you may be accidentally training yourself to think you'll have a second chance when you really don't. When you perform for a live audience, you have to do your trick perfectly the first time.

Thirty minutes of practice might not seem like a lot of time, but there is a hidden benefit to this approach. Having such a short rehearsal time forces you to try your best the first time and prepares you more effectively for a live performance. After working on one skill, you can then move on to the next one you are practicing. If you stumble, it's best to roll with it and try to improve on the next take. This attitude also keeps you thinking on your feet and is great training for performing in front of a live audience.

SET THE SCENE

Nothing can quite get us in the mood for practicing like the right atmosphere. I am lucky enough to have an extra room as a mini studio where I can practice. Surrounding myself with puppetry keeps me motivated and sets the mood when I walk into the room. Your space might include posters, images, puppets and other trinkets that show your love for puppetry in all its glory. Having a dedicated space for your puppetry is extremely helpful because it also allows you to have your camera and puppets ready to go at a moment's notice, which lets you spend less time setting up and more time practicing. Otherwise, that set-up time just cuts into your practice time.

However, a dedicated space is not a necessity; it's just a "nice-to-have." You can turn any space into a perfect place to practice your puppetry. Changing locations may help for some themes, too. Imagine the inspiration of a setting like a kitchen or the possibilities for stories in a musty garage. There is built-in inspiration right there!

Here are a few more tips for making your space practice-friendly:

- Remove any distractions.
- Ask family members to keep noise levels low.
- Put your phone on silent and out of reach.

KEEP A RECORD

After hours of practicing, you may ask yourself, "am I really getting anywhere?" To stop this doubtful train in its tracks, keep a journal or log containing all your small achievements. In this journal, you can track milestones and goals achieved.

Another great way to track your progress is to record every practice session. It will be very rewarding to look back at these videos years later to see how far you have come. Video files can take up a lot of space, though. To open up space in your camera, you can upload your footage to YouTube as private videos. There are multiple benefits to using YouTube: first, it's free storage. Second, the footage is time-stamped and organized in chronological order. And finally, it's easy to access anywhere you have an internet connection. Also, with YouTube, you don't have to worry about losing your footage if your computer crashes.

As an added bonus, if you want to make your videos public, you can easily bring an audience along for the ride. Many of those who undertake self-improvement and skill perfecting these days start blogs or vlogs to "hold themselves accountable." If you think this sort of thing might keep you on the right track, then why not give it a try? For many, this can be a great way to stay motivated.

GIVE YOURSELF A BREAK

It's easy to get swept up in practicing and find yourself on the verge of burnout, and that's one of the quickest ways to fall out of love with your dream. So if you need a rest, take one – you've earned it. And, if you find yourself becoming particularly frustrated or distressed with your practice sessions, take a step back, breathe, and come back to it later. What really matters is that you don't give up.

There's a world of greatness and improvement right at your fingertips. You already have what it takes to be the best; all that's left is to put it into practice! So what are you waiting for? You've got this!

CHAPTER 8 TAKEAWAYS

- Practicing regularly is the only way you will see improvement, and keeping a routine will help you make time to practice.

- Though repetition can be helpful, practicing cold can really sharpen your skills.

- Since you are practicing in front of a camera anyway, hit record! Document your growth.

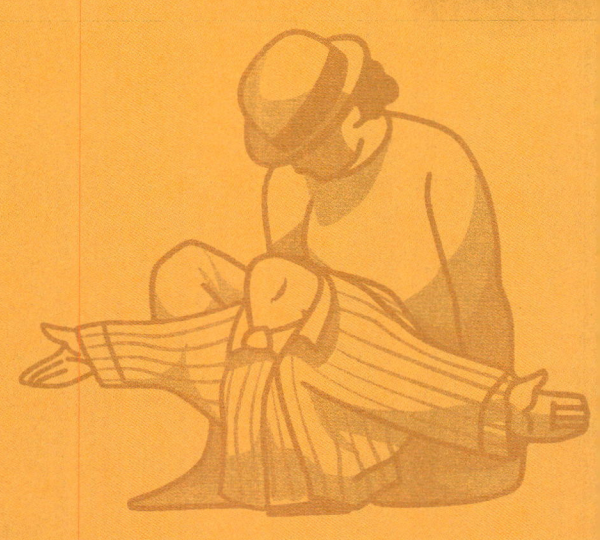

CHAPTER 9
PROMOTION

In the age of digital marketing, it's easier than ever to promote your show to the public. However, the concept of promoting your show can feel daunting and out of reach. If you are creating a web show on social media, the best way to promote it is with the content itself. Consistently making content on a regular schedule gives your audience a reason to keep coming back. Everyone wants followers, but if you are not making regularly scheduled content… well, what is there to follow?

There is a common mistake I see a lot of people make when trying to promote a puppet show online. They forget to keep their social media "social." Many people try to treat it too much like a traditional television media show, which is a one-way relationship. The point of social media is to be SOCIAL (as in *interactive*). And you do this by building a two-way relationship with your audience. Not only do you want them to interact with your video, but you need to interact with them by responding to their comments, or even having your character make a video response to some of the comments. This approach makes people feel invested in your material, and also gives them more reasons to keep coming back; it lets your audience grow with you.

LIVE SHOWS

If your show is a live event, here are a few tips that go beyond designing posters and posting them all over town. First is the framing of your show. Don't think of it as just a show; you want to create an event. Make the focus of your advertising about the audience, not about the show. Market it as the highlight of the week for your audience, such as a night out or a time for the family to bond. This type of marketing makes your show more than just an hour with puppets in a theatre. It makes it a way for your audience to create a memory with loved ones.

The Lion King on Broadway does not hide the fact that they use puppets, but even so, it's not promoted as a "puppet show." Puppetry is the medium, not the attraction. It's the same for animation. Pixar doesn't promote its movies by advertising the best animation. They are famous for being able to tell compelling stories. Thus, to attract people to your show, promote an experience and the fact that you are telling compelling stories, not the puppetry.

MAKE A PROMO VIDEO

They say a picture is worth 1,000 words. At thirty frames per second, a video is a lot of "pictures" and can really hook your audience if done right. Everyone loves an intriguing video. Draw in the crowd by making a quick 15-30 second promotional video for your show. Start with something that can really grab people's attention, such as a question or an interesting fact. Use "backstage" clips or footage from the dress rehearsal to add to the intrigue and make viewers feel more invested in the process.

LET THE WORLD KNOW!

What's the best way to spread the word about your show? Talk about it! This is sometimes hard for people because they don't want to come off as bragging or self-indulgent. But if *you* aren't willing to talk about your show, why would you expect other people to talk about it?

What you really want to do is share your excitement. So don't be afraid to message people. Reaching out individually to people you know that may be interested adds a unique personal touch, as long as you do it sincerely. This means no "copy and paste" messages. Spamming people with template-style messages will most likely have the opposite effect from the one you want. People are more likely to attend if you make them feel special with a personal message, and they're also more likely to share your promotion with others and spread the news about your show.

You have endless places to promote your show using the internet. Try out multiple forms of marketing and find what works for you. People want to come to your show; they just don't know the details until you promote it.

CHAPTER 9 TAKEAWAYS

- Make your social media posts feel authentic. Do not overproduce your posts, or they will feel like an ad.

- Make your promotions about the audience experience, not the medium or the premise.

- Talk about your show! If you won't talk about it, why would you expect anyone else to?

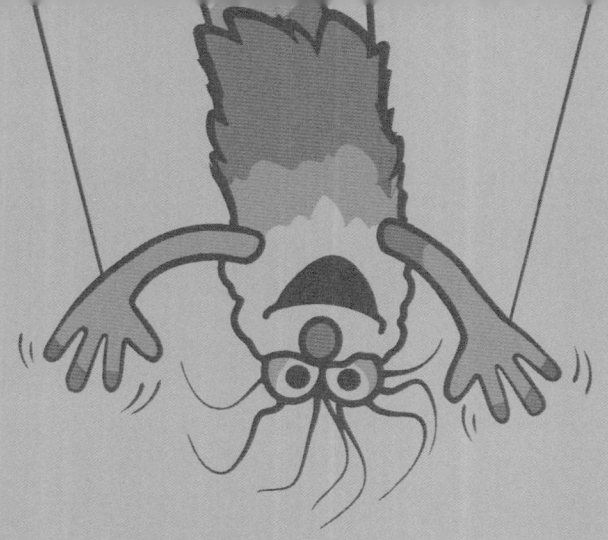

CHAPTER 10
JOIN THE COMMUNITY

The puppetry community is wonderful. It has brought together some of the most kind and generous people I have ever met. People who are willing to share their techniques and experiences. People who are willing to support and share each other's work. People who are willing to share their knowledge of puppet history.

There are many ways to get involved. Depending on where you live in the world, there are many different avenues to make connections. If possible, get involved locally. Many areas in the world even have local puppetry guilds, and if there isn't one in your area, YOU CAN START ONE!!! Start making friends and discover other forms of puppetry.

If you live in the Americas, I highly recommend joining "Puppeteers Of America" (PofA). The PofA is a non-profit organization founded in 1937. They organize The National Puppetry Festival, which I also highly recommend. There are a lot of benefits to becoming a member of Puppeteers Of America, but one of my favorites is the "Puppetry Journal" that comes out quarterly. It's a great way to learn more about puppetry and connect with other puppeteers.

To connect with the global puppet community, there is an international puppetry organization called UNIMA that was founded in 1929 and has members in many countries. Its members contribute to the development and dissemination of puppetry works around the world. UNIMA also has a puppetry magazine. I am a member of both!

Another great source of community for this style of puppetry is the Puppet Nerd Facebook Group. This group has members who post daily, showing off puppets they are building and shows they are working on. It's also a great place to get advice and ask questions. There is also the Puppet Maker's Workshop Facebook Group, which is also great for other styles of puppetry.

These groups are just the tip of the iceberg. There are many other notable groups and opportunities for getting involved in the puppetry community. Many more are listed in the "resources section" at the end of the book; be sure to check them out.

The art of puppetry is the act of a lifetime. Just like you never stop being a friend, you never truly stop being a puppeteer. It has a knack for finding a spot in your heart and setting up shop for, well, forever.

Puppetry is for everyone. It has transformed lives by bringing fun, laughter, and good memories to audiences and the puppeteer alike. This book is more than a guide into puppetry, making your characters, and putting on a show; It's an open invitation to join one of the coolest, most diverse communities filled with some of the most wonderful humans you'll ever meet. The puppetry community will offer you relentless support as you grow. Puppetry is a medium of expression; whether you seek to start a puppet company or just make it a hobby, getting started in puppetry is a choice that transforms your life for the better.

I hope this book has given you some inspiration to start or continue your journey in puppetry. There is so much left to explore and create. And I can't wait to see what you come up with. Now… go make a puppet show!!!

Nuff said,

Adam Kreutinger

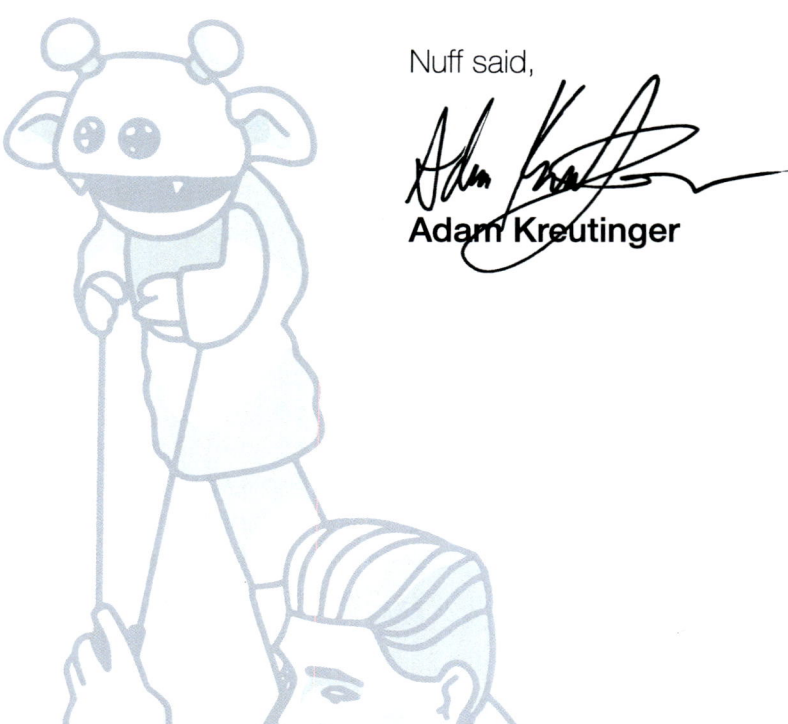

ADDENDUM

PUPPETRY ORGANIZATIONS

The Jim Henson Foundation | HensonFoundation.org
Center For Puppetry Arts | Puppet.org
Puppeteers Of America | Puppeteers.org
UNIMA | UNIMA.org

HIGHER EDUCATION

UConn Puppet Arts, *BFA and MA/MFA Programs*
www.drama.uconn.edu/programs/puppet-arts

West Virginia University, *BFA Program*
https://admissions.wvu.edu/academics/majors/puppetry

PUPPET MAKING

Supplies | www.PuppetNerd.com/supplies
Supplies | www.PuppetThings.com
Tutorials | www.PuppetCrafts.com
Puppet Maker's Workshop | PuppetMakersWorkshop.com
Simple Puppet | SnoofsOfTheWorld.com/make-a-snoof

PUPPET PATTERNS

www.FreePuppetPatterns.com
www.ProjectPuppet.com
www.PuppetNerd.com

ONLINE CHAT GROUPS

Puppet Nerd Tutorial Q&A | PuppetryConnects.com
Puppet Makers Workshop | Search on Facebook

PUPPETRY PODCASTS

Below the Frame | BelowTheFrame.buzzsprout.com
Puppet Tears Podcast | PuppetTears.com
Under the Puppet | SaturdayMorningMedia.com
Puppet Podcast | PuppetPodcast.com

WORKSHOPS & TRAINING

Beyond the Sock | BeyondTheSock.unt.edu
Little Shadow Academy | LittleShadowProductions.com
The National Puppetry Conference at the Eugene O'Neill Theater Center | TheOneill.org/PUP

PUPPETRY FUN!

Kids' Camp | CampPuppet.com
Good Reads | PuppetVision.blog
Crafts and Shows | WondersparkPuppets.com
The Power of Puppetry | CamGarrity.com/Puppetry
All Things Puppet Nerd | Puppetry101.com
Monitor Practice & Downloadable Background Images | ThePuppetClub.com

FESTIVALS & EVENTS

The National Puppetry Festival
Chicago International Puppet Theater Festival
New York State Puppet Festival
World Puppetry Day | Celebrate on March 21st

PUPPET RENTALS

Swazzle Puppet Studio | Swazzle.com
Monkey Boys Productions | MonkeyBoysProductions.com

VENUES, MUSEUMS, & EXHIBITS

The Ballard Institute | Storrs, CT
The Center for Puppetry Arts | Atlanta, GA
The Museum of Moving Image | Astoria, NY
Puppet Showplace Theater | Brookline, MA
Strong Museum of Play | Rochester, NY

PUPPET SHOPS & STUDIOS

Cinemarionette | @cinemarionette
Figurenschneider | @figurenschneider
Furry Puppet Studio | @furrypuppet
Handspring Puppet Company | @handspringpuppetco123
IBEX Puppetry | @ibexpuppetry
Pro Puppet Makers | @propuppetmakers
Puppet Heap | @puppetheap
The Puppet Kitchen | @thepuppetkitchen
Screen Novelties | @screennovelties
Significant Object | @significant.object
Viva La Puppet | @vivalapuppet

Made in the USA
Monee, IL
16 September 2023

42216316R00069